The Road

A Raw Tale of Wandering, Hunger & the Harsh
Realities of Life on the American Frontier

A Modern Translation
Adapted for the Contemporary Reader

Jack London

Translated by Tim Zengerink

Table of Contents

Preface
Message to the Reader

Rebuilding the Greatest Library in Human History

Thousands of years ago, the Library of Alexandria was the heart of global knowledge — a sanctuary where the wisdom of every known civilization was gathered and shared freely.

And then, it was lost.

Now, we're rebuilding it — and you are invited to join us.

At the Library of Alexandria, we've set out to make every book available to every person on Earth — not just in print, but in every language, every format, and for every reader.

Here's how we do it:

- **Deluxe Print Editions at True Printing Cost** - Order any book as a high-quality paperback, elegant hardcover, or stunning boxset — and only pay what it costs to print. No markups. No middlemen.
- **Unlimited Access to the Greatest Works** - Enjoy thousands of timeless classics — from Plato to Shakespeare to Tolstoy — in beautiful, modern eBook and audiobook editions. Read and listen without limits — for every reader, everywhere.
- **Modern Translations for Every Language & Dialect** - We're reimagining the classics in clear, accessible language — and translating them into every dialect imaginable. Everyone deserves to understand humanity's greatest ideas.

When you visit **LibraryofAlexandria.com**, you're not just accessing books — you're joining a global movement to restore, preserve, and share the wisdom of civilization.

Join us today at LibraryofAlexandria.com

Together, we'll ensure the light of human wisdom never fades again.

With gratitude,

The Modern Library of Alexandria Team

Visit:
www.libraryofalexandria.com
Or scan the code below:

Introduction

Jack London's Journey into
the Margins of America

In *The Road*, Jack London departs from the wilderness of the Yukon and ventures into a different kind of frontier—the rugged and often invisible landscapes of early 20th-century America, where itinerant workers, tramps, and hobos traveled the country in search of survival, adventure, and fleeting opportunities. First published in 1907, this autobiographical collection of essays and stories captures London's experiences during the economic depression of the 1890s, when he took to the rails as a young man and lived as a vagabond. It is a raw, unfiltered portrait of life on the move, marked by hunger, cold, danger, and moments of unexpected humanity.

Unlike many of London's more famous works, which are fictional narratives shaped around strong, central characters and dramatic plots, *The Road* reads like a memoir interspersed with adventure stories, keen social observations, and biting commentary on the economic structures of his time. Here, London is both narrator and protagonist, recounting how, as a teenager, he abandoned conventional life to join the ranks of America's wandering underclass. These travels took him through cities, small towns, and wilderness stretches, offering an intimate glimpse into a world that most middle-class readers of the time neither saw nor understood.

The America that London depicts in *The Road* is an America in transition. Industrialization was transforming the economy, but vast sections of the population—particularly working-class men—

2

found themselves without stable jobs or homes. The railroads, which were both the lifelines and the barriers of this era, became the means by which thousands of men, including London, roamed from one part of the country to another. Life on the rails was not romantic; it was brutal, physically punishing, and fraught with dangers ranging from starvation to arrest. London's stories pull no punches in describing the harsh realities of this existence.

Yet there is also an undeniable vitality and adventure in *The Road*. London's prose brings to life the camaraderie among fellow travelers, the cunning required to evade railroad guards (the notorious "bulls"), and the resilience needed to survive when resources were scarce. His depictions are often humorous, sometimes tragic, and always infused with a sense of restless energy. London understood that while life on *The Road* was difficult, it was also liberating in ways that conventional society could never be.

Reading *The Road* is like stepping into a time capsule of pre-World War I America, but it is also a timeless meditation on freedom, poverty, and survival. It challenges readers to consider the social and economic systems that force people to live at the margins, while also celebrating the ingenuity and spirit of those who endure. For modern readers, it offers not just a historical account but a set of enduring truths about human resilience and the quest for meaning in difficult circumstances.

This introduction aims to provide both context and interpretation for *The Road*, preparing the reader to appreciate London's work in its full depth. We will explore the autobiographical roots of the book, its major themes of survival and social critique, and its enduring legacy in American literature. Understanding the man behind the narrative—Jack London himself—is essential, for *The Road* is as much about London's personal journey as it is about the collective experiences of the itinerant workers he encountered.

Themes of Freedom, Hardship, and Social Critique

One of the most compelling aspects of *The Road* is its exploration of freedom. For London, the life of a hobo represented a paradoxical mix of deprivation and liberation. On the one hand, traveling the country without money, shelter, or security meant constant physical hardship. Hunger was a daily companion, and finding food often required a mix of charm, trickery, and sheer luck. Arrests were frequent, and many towns treated itinerant workers as criminals simply for existing. Yet, on the other hand, this life on *The Road* offered a kind of freedom that few conventional jobs or social roles could provide.

London writes about this freedom with both admiration and ambivalence. He portrays the hobo life as a rebellion against the rigid structures of industrial capitalism, where men were often reduced to mere cogs in the economic machine. On the rails, however, one could move freely from place to place, unbound by schedules, bosses, or societal expectations. This freedom, however, came at a cost, forcing individuals to confront their own endurance, intelligence, and capacity for survival.

Another prominent theme in *The Road* is the stark reality of poverty. London does not romanticize hunger or homelessness. He vividly describes the physical toll of sleeping in the cold, walking miles with empty stomachs, and facing the hostility of both nature and society. His accounts of "jungle" camps—makeshift settlements where hobos gathered to rest and share food—paint a picture of a community forged in hardship, where camaraderie and mutual aid were essential for survival. These scenes are both heartwarming and heartbreaking, as they reveal the resilience of the human spirit in the face of systemic neglect.

London's social critique is sharp and unapologetic. He exposes the cruelty of the legal system, which often criminalized poverty rather than addressing its causes. His descriptions of chain gangs, harsh prison conditions, and the arbitrary power of local authorities are not just anecdotes—they are indictments of a society that punished the vulnerable instead of supporting them. In this way, *The Road* can be seen as an early work of social realism, highlighting the structural inequalities that shaped American life at the turn of the century.

Yet London also celebrates the ingenuity and courage of those who lived this life. The hobos he encounters are not merely victims but survivors—resourceful individuals who navigate a hostile world with creativity and determination. Through his encounters with these men, London learns lessons about adaptability, solidarity, and the value of experience over theory. This emphasis on lived experience is a hallmark of London's writing, reflecting his own belief that true knowledge comes from engaging with the world rather than observing it from a distance.

The Legacy of
The Road and Jack London's Voice

The Road occupies a unique place in Jack London's body of work. While he is best known for adventure stories like *The Call of the Wild* and *White Fang*, which explore the relationship between humans, animals, and the natural world, *The Road* is firmly grounded in human society. It is a work of reportage as much as storytelling, blending autobiographical detail with narrative flair. In many ways, it anticipates the later tradition of literary journalism, where writers like George Orwell and John Steinbeck would document the lives of the working class with similar attention to detail and empathy.

For readers today, *The Road* offers not just a glimpse into the past but an enduring exploration of themes that remain relevant. Issues of economic inequality, homelessness, and the search for dignity in difficult circumstances are as pressing now as they were in London's time. His observations about the fragility of social safety nets and the arbitrary nature of authority resonate in contemporary discussions about poverty and justice.

London's style in *The Road* is characteristically vivid and direct. His prose captures the rhythms of speech, the sharpness of sensory detail, and the immediacy of lived experience. When he describes the clatter of train wheels, the taste of stale bread, or the bitter chill of a winter night, the reader feels transported into his world. His voice is both confident and conversational, inviting the reader to share in his adventures while also reflecting on their deeper significance.

As you read *The Road*, consider the ways in which London balances personal narrative with social observation. Pay attention to his use of humor—often dark, sometimes ironic—to underscore the absurdities of life on the margins. Notice how he portrays the characters he meets, not as faceless drifters but as individuals with unique stories, personalities, and dreams. This humanizing approach is one of the book's greatest strengths, transforming what could have been a mere travelogue into a profound exploration of humanity.

In conclusion, *The Road* is more than a memoir of hardship; it is a testament to the resilience of the human spirit and the enduring quest for freedom. Jack London's journey through the American frontier of the rails is both deeply personal and universally resonant, inviting readers to reflect on their own relationship with society, work, and survival. As you embark on this reading, prepare to encounter not just the grit and hunger of life on *The Road*, but also the moments of unexpected beauty, kindness, and insight that make London's work timeless.

Coming Clean

There's a woman in Nevada who I lied to constantly, consistently, and without shame for several hours. I don't want to apologize to her. That's not my intention at all. But I do want to explain what happened. Unfortunately, I don't know her name, let alone where she lives now. If she happens to read this, I hope she'll reach out to me.

It was in Reno, Nevada, during the summer of 1892. It was also fair time, and the town was packed with small-time criminals and cheap gamblers, not to mention a massive and starving crowd of homeless drifters. It was these starving drifters who made the town a "hungry" place. They begged at the back doors of residents' homes until those back doors stopped answering.

A tough town for "scoffings," was what the hoboes called it back then. I know I went without many meals, despite being able to "throw my feet" with anyone when it came to "slamming a gate" for a "poke-out" or a "set-down," or asking for a "light piece" on the street. I was so desperate in that town one day that I slipped past the porter and snuck into the private railroad car of some traveling millionaire. The train began moving just as I reached the platform, and I rushed toward the millionaire with the porter one step behind, reaching for me. It was a tie, because I reached the millionaire at the exact same moment the porter caught up to me. I had no time for polite conversation. "Give me a quarter for food," I said quickly. And I swear, that millionaire reached into his pocket and handed me exactly a quarter. I'm convinced he was so shocked that he responded without thinking, and I've regretted ever since that I didn't ask him for a dollar. I know he would have given it to me. I jumped off the platform of that private car while the porter tried to kick me in the face. He missed. You're at a serious disadvantage when you're trying to jump from the bottom step of a train car without breaking your neck on the tracks, while an angry railroad worker on the platform above is trying to kick you in the face with his size eleven boot. But I got that quarter! I got it!

But to return to the woman I lied to so shamelessly. This happened on the evening of my final day in Reno. I had spent the day at the racetrack watching the horses run and had missed my dinner, which was the main meal at midday. I was starving, and on top of that, a committee of public safety had just formed to drive people like me—hungry drifters—out of town. The police had already rounded up many of my fellow hoboes, and I could hear the warm valleys of California calling to me from beyond the cold peaks of the Sierra Nevada mountains. I had two things left to do before leaving Reno behind for good. First, I needed to catch the blind baggage car on the westbound train that night. Second, and more immediately, I had to find something to eat. Even a young person would think twice about riding all night on an empty stomach, clinging to the outside of a train racing through snowsheds, tunnels, and the endless snows of towering mountains.

But finding something to eat proved to be a difficult challenge. I was rejected at a dozen houses. Sometimes I received insulting comments and was told about the jail cell that should be mine if I got what I deserved. The worst part was that such claims were all too accurate. That was why I was heading west that night. The police were out in the town, actively searching for the hungry and homeless, since those were the people who filled the jail cells.

At other homes, doors were slammed shut right in front of me, abruptly ending my courteous and modest plea for food. At one residence, they refused to open the door entirely. I remained on the porch knocking while they peered at me through the glass. They even lifted up a robust young boy so he could see over the adults' shoulders to get a look at the vagrant who wouldn't be receiving any meal at their home.

It started to seem like I would have to turn to the very poor for my meals. The very poor are the last reliable refuge for a hungry wanderer. You can always count on the very poor. They never refuse food to someone who's hungry. Time after time, all across the United States, I've been denied food by the grand house on the hill; yet I've always been given food from the small shack down by the creek or marsh, with its broken windows patched with rags and its weary-faced mother worn down by hard work. Oh, you charity peddlers! Go to the poor and learn, because only the poor are truly charitable. They don't give or hold back from their surplus. They have no surplus. They give, and they never hold back, from what they need for themselves, and very often from what they desperately need for themselves. Throwing a bone to the dog isn't charity. Charity is sharing the bone with the dog when you're just as hungry as the dog.

There was one house in particular where I was rejected that evening. The porch windows looked into the dining room, and through them I could see a man eating pie—a large meat pie. I stood in the open doorway, and while he spoke with me, he continued eating. He was wealthy, and from his wealth had grown bitterness toward his less fortunate fellow men.

He interrupted my request for food, sharply declaring, "I don't think you actually want to work."

Now this didn't matter. I hadn't mentioned anything about work. The subject I had brought up was "food." Actually, I didn't want to work. I wanted to catch the westbound train that evening.

"You wouldn't work if you had a chance," he bullied.

I looked at his gentle-faced wife and realized that if this guard dog weren't here, I'd take a shot at that meat pie myself. But the guard dog was devouring the pie, and I could see that I'd have to appease him if I wanted to get any of it. So I sighed inwardly and went along with his work ethic.

"Of course I want work," I lied.

"Don't believe it," he snorted.

"Test me," I replied, getting caught up in the bluff.

"All right," he said. "Come to the corner of blank and blank streets"—I've forgotten the exact address—"tomorrow morning. You know where that burned building is, and I'll put you to work throwing bricks."

"All right, sir; I'll be there."

He grunted and continued eating. I waited. After a few minutes he looked up with an expression that said he thought I had left, and asked:—

"Well?"

"I... I'm waiting for something to eat," I said softly.

"I knew you wouldn't work!" he shouted.

He was correct, naturally; however, his conclusion must have come from reading minds, since his reasoning couldn't support it. But someone asking for help at the door must remain humble, so I accepted his reasoning just as I had accepted his moral principles.

"You see, I'm hungry right now," I said, still speaking gently. "Tomorrow morning I'll be even hungrier. Just imagine how hungry I'll be after throwing bricks around all day without having anything to eat. Now if you give me something to eat, I'll be in great shape to handle those bricks."

He seriously thought about my request while continuing to eat, as his wife almost started to speak in an apologetic way but held back.

"I'll tell you what I'll do," he said while eating. "Come to work tomorrow, and around midday I'll give you an advance for your dinner. That will show whether you're serious or not."

"Meanwhile—" I started to say, but he cut me off.

"If I gave you something to eat right now, I'd never see you again. Oh, I know your type. Look at me. I don't owe anyone anything. I have never sunk so low as to ask anyone for food. I have always earned my meals. The problem with you is that you're lazy and immoral. I can see it written all over your face. I have worked hard and lived honestly. I have made myself into what I am today. And you can do the same thing, if you work hard and live honestly."

"Like you?" I asked.

Unfortunately, no hint of humor had ever reached into the dark, work-consumed spirit of that man.

"Yes, like me," he answered.

"All of us?" I asked.

"Yes, all of you," he answered, his voice filled with unwavering certainty.

"But if everyone became like you," I said, "let me point out that there wouldn't be anyone left to throw bricks for you."

I'm certain I caught a hint of amusement in his wife's eyes. As for him, he looked absolutely horrified—though whether he was shocked by the terrible prospect of a reformed society where he couldn't find anyone willing to throw bricks for him, or by my boldness, I'll never be able to tell.

"I won't waste my words on you," he roared. "Get out of here, you ungrateful brat!"

I shuffled my feet to signal that I was planning to leave, and asked:—

"And I don't get anything to eat?"

He suddenly stood up. He was a big man. I was a stranger in an unfamiliar place, and John Law was searching for me. I left quickly. "But why ungrateful?" I wondered as I slammed his gate shut. "What on earth did he give me to be ungrateful for?" I glanced back. I could still see him through the window. He had gone back to his pie.

By this point, I had become discouraged. I walked past numerous houses without daring to approach them. Every house appeared the same, and none seemed "promising." After covering several blocks on foot, I shook off my dejection and summoned my courage. This whole business of asking for food was nothing more than a game, and if I didn't care for the hand I'd been dealt, I could always ask for new cards. I decided to try the next house. I walked up to it in the growing dusk, making my way around to the kitchen door.

I knocked gently, and when I saw the kind face of the middle-aged woman who answered, inspiration struck me with the "story" I needed to tell. You have to understand that a beggar's success depends entirely on his ability to tell a compelling story. First and foremost, in that very instant, the beggar must "size up" his target. After that, he must tell a story that will connect with the specific personality and temperament of that particular person. And this is where the real challenge lies: in the same moment he's evaluating his target, he must begin his story. There's no time allowed for preparation. Like a flash of lightning, he must understand the nature of the person and create a tale that will strike home. The successful hobo must be an artist. He must create spontaneously and instantly—and not based on a theme chosen from the wealth of his own imagination, but on the theme he reads in the face of whoever opens the door, whether it's a man, woman, or child, sweet or bitter, generous or stingy, good-natured or bad-tempered, Jew or Gentile, black or white, prejudiced or accepting, narrow-minded or open, or whatever else they might be. I've often thought that much of my success as a story-writer comes from this training during my vagrant days. To get the food I needed to survive, I was forced to tell tales that sounded genuine. At the back door, out of harsh necessity, you develop the persuasiveness and authenticity that all experts on short-story writing emphasize. Also, I'm quite certain it was my apprenticeship as a tramp that turned me into a realist. Realism is the only currency you can trade at the kitchen door for food.

After all, art is simply masterful skill, and skill can rescue many a "story." I recall lying in a police station in Winnipeg, Manitoba. I was traveling west on the Canadian Pacific Railway. Naturally, the police wanted to hear my story, so I gave them one— improvised on the spot. They were people of the land, living in the heart of the continent, so what better tale to tell them than one of the sea? They would never be able to catch me in a lie about that. And so I spun a heartbreaking story about my life aboard the brutal ship Glenmore. (I had once spotted the Glenmore anchored in San Francisco Bay.)

I was an English apprentice, I explained. But they pointed out that I didn't sound like an English boy. I had to come up with something on the spot. I had been born and raised in the United States. When my parents died, I had been sent to England to live with my grandparents. They were the ones who had arranged my apprenticeship on the Glenmore. I hope the captain of the Glenmore will forgive me, because I painted quite a picture of him that night in the Winnipeg police station. Such cruelty! Such brutality! Such devilish cleverness in torture! It explained why I had abandoned the Glenmore in Montreal.

But why was I traveling west through the middle of Canada when my grandparents lived in England? I quickly invented a married sister who lived in California. She would look after me. I elaborated extensively on her caring personality. However, those tough policemen weren't finished with me yet. I had signed onto the Glenmore in England; during the two years that had passed before I jumped ship in Montreal, what had the Glenmore been doing and where had she sailed? So I took those land-dwelling officers on a journey around the globe with me. Battered by crashing waves and pelted with ocean spray, they battled a typhoon alongside me off Japan's coast. They helped me load and unload freight in every port across the Seven Seas. I brought them to India, Rangoon, and China, and had them chip ice with me around Cape Horn before finally dropping anchor in Montreal.

And then they told me to wait a moment, and one police officer went out into the night while I warmed myself by the stove, constantly trying to figure out what trap they were planning to set for me.

I groaned inwardly when I watched him enter through the door behind the police officer. No wandering gypsy's mischief had placed those small golden rings in his ears; no winds from the plains had weathered that skin into creased leather; and neither snowdrifts nor mountain slopes had given his gait that distinctive swaying motion. When those eyes met mine, I recognized the unmistakable sun-bleached look of the ocean. Here stood a story, unfortunately, with half a dozen officers watching me take it in— me, who had never navigated the China seas, never rounded Cape Horn, never set eyes on India or Rangoon.

I was desperate. Disaster loomed ahead of me, taking the shape of that gold-earringed, weathered sailor. Who could he be? What did he represent? I had to figure him out before he figured me out. I needed to find a new direction, or those corrupt officers would direct me straight to a jail cell, a courtroom, and even more cells. If he interrogated me first, before I understood how much he already knew, I would be finished.

But did I reveal my desperate situation to those sharp-eyed protectors of Winnipeg's public safety? Absolutely not. I greeted that old sailor with bright eyes and a beaming smile, showing all the fake relief that a drowning person would display when grabbing a life preserver in their final desperate moment. Here was someone who understood and who would confirm my real story to those detective-like investigators who didn't understand, or at least that's what I tried to act out. I grabbed onto him; I bombarded him with questions about his life. In front of my judges, I would establish the credibility of my rescuer before he could rescue me.

He was a gentle sailor—someone easily taken advantage of.

14

The police officers became restless as I continued questioning him. Finally, one of them ordered me to be quiet. I fell silent; however, while I stayed quiet, my mind was actively working, developing the plan for what would happen next. I had gathered sufficient information to proceed. He was French. He had always worked aboard French commercial ships, except for one trip on a British vessel. And most importantly—what wonderful news!—he hadn't been at sea for twenty years.

The police officer encouraged him to take a closer look at me.

"You stopped in Rangoon?" he asked.

I nodded. "We left our third mate on shore there. He had a fever."

If he had asked me what type of fever it was, I would have said "Enteric," even though I had absolutely no idea what enteric meant. But he didn't ask me that. Instead, his next question was:—

"And how is Rangoon?"

"All right. It rained a whole lot when we were there."

"Did you get shore leave?"

"Sure," I replied. "Three of us apprentices went ashore together."

"Do you remember the temple?"

"Which temple?" I shot back.

"The large one at the top of the stairs."

If I recalled that temple, I understood I would need to describe it. The chasm opened before me.

I shook my head.

"You can see it from anywhere in the harbor," he told me. "You don't need to go ashore to see that temple."

I have never despised a temple so much in my entire life. However, I repaired that specific temple in Rangoon.

"You can't see it from the harbor," I argued. "You can't see it from the town. You can't see it from the top of the stairway. Because—"I stopped for dramatic effect. "Because there isn't any temple there."

"But I saw it with my own eyes!" he cried.

"When was that?" I asked.

"Seventy-one."

"It was destroyed in the great earthquake of 1887," I explained. "It was very old."

There was a pause. He was busy rebuilding in his aged eyes the young man's vision of that beautiful temple by the sea.

"The stairway is still there," I helped him remember. "You can see it from anywhere in the harbor. And do you remember that small island on the right side when you're coming into the harbor?" I figured there must have been one there (I was ready to move it to the left side if needed), because he nodded in agreement. "It's gone," I told him. "There's seven fathoms of water there now."

I had gained a moment to catch my breath. While he reflected on how time had changed things, I prepared the final details of my story.

"Do you remember the customs house in Bombay?"

He remembered it.

"Burned to the ground," I announced.

"Do you remember Jim Wan?" he shot back at me.

"Dead," I said, though I had absolutely no idea who the hell Jim Wan was.

I was on thin ice again.

"Do you remember Billy Harper, from Shanghai?" I asked him quickly.

That old sailor tried hard to remember, but the Billy Harper I had imagined was beyond what his faded memory could recall.

"Of course you remember Billy Harper," I insisted. "Everyone knows him. He's been working there for forty years. Well, he's still there, that's all."

And then something miraculous occurred. The sailor recalled

Billy Harper. There might have been a real Billy Harper, and he might have spent forty years in Shanghai and still been living there, but this was completely new information to me.

For a full thirty minutes more, the sailor and I continued our conversation in the same way. Eventually he convinced the police officers that I was exactly who I claimed to be, and after spending the night in jail and eating breakfast, I was set free to continue my journey west to visit my married sister in San Francisco.

But to return to the woman in Reno who opened her door to me in the deepening twilight. At the first glimpse of her kindly face I took my cue. I became a sweet, innocent, unfortunate young man. I couldn't speak. I opened my mouth and closed it again. Never in my life before had I asked anyone for food. My embarrassment was painful, extreme. I was ashamed. I, who looked upon begging as a delightful whim, transformed myself into a true son of conventional society, burdened with all its middle-class morality. Only the harsh pangs of hunger could compel me to do something so degraded and disgraceful as beg for food. And into my face I tried to put all the pale longing of starved and naive youth unaccustomed to begging.

"You're hungry, my poor boy," she said.

I had gotten her to speak first.

I nodded and swallowed hard.

"This is the first time I've ever... asked," I stammered.

"Come right in." The door swung open. "We've already finished eating, but the fire is still burning and I can prepare something for you."

She examined me carefully once she brought me into the light.

"I wish my son were as healthy and strong as you are," she said. "But he isn't strong. He falls down sometimes. He just fell this afternoon and hurt himself badly, the poor thing."

She spoke to him with a motherly voice, filled with an

17

indescribable tenderness that I longed to claim for myself. I looked over at him. He sat on the other side of the table, thin and pale, his head wrapped in bandages. He remained perfectly still, but his eyes, gleaming in the lamplight, were locked on me with an unwavering and curious gaze.

"Just like my poor father," I said. "He suffered from epilepsy. Some kind of dizziness. It baffled the doctors. They could never figure out what was wrong with him."

"Is he dead?" she asked softly, placing half a dozen soft-boiled eggs in front of me.

"Dead," I swallowed hard. "Two weeks ago. I was there when it happened. We were crossing the street together. He collapsed right there on the spot. He never regained consciousness. They carried him into a drugstore. That's where he died."

And so I shared the heartbreaking story of my father—how, following my mother's passing, he and I had traveled to San Francisco from the ranch; how his pension (he was a former soldier), along with the small amount of other money he possessed, wasn't sufficient; and how he had attempted to make a living selling books door-to-door. Additionally, I recounted my own hardships during the several days following his death when I had wandered alone and abandoned on the streets of San Francisco. While that kind woman heated up biscuits, prepared bacon, and made additional eggs, and while I matched her pace in consuming everything she set in front of me, I expanded the image of that unfortunate orphan boy and added more specifics. I became that unfortunate boy. I had faith in him just as I had faith in the delicious eggs I was consuming. I could have cried for myself. I'm certain the tears did creep into my voice occasionally. It was quite compelling.

In fact, with every touch I added to the picture, that kind soul gave me something as well. She prepared a lunch for me to take with me. She packed many boiled eggs, pepper and salt, and other items, along with a large apple. She supplied me with three pairs of thick red wool socks. She gave me clean handkerchiefs and other things that I've forgotten since then. And the entire time she kept cooking more and more while I kept eating more and more. I ate like a wild animal; but it was a long journey across the Sierras on a freight train, and I had no idea when or where I would find my next meal. And throughout it all, like a grim reminder at a celebration, silent and still, her own unfortunate son sat and stared at me from across the table. I imagine I represented mystery, romance, and adventure to him—everything that was denied to the weak spark of life within him. And yet I couldn't help wondering, once or twice, whether he could see right through me to the depths of my dishonest heart.

"But where are you going?" she asked me.

"Salt Lake City," I said. "I have a sister there—a married sister." (I wondered whether I should make her out to be a Mormon, and decided against it.) "Her husband is a plumber—a plumbing contractor."

Now I understood that plumbing contractors were typically known for earning substantial incomes. However, I had already committed myself. It was my responsibility to prove myself worthy.

"They would have sent me the money for my fare if I had asked for it," I explained, "but they've been dealing with illness and business problems. His partner cheated him. So I didn't want to write asking for money. I knew I could find a way to get there somehow. I let them believe I had enough to reach Salt Lake City. She's wonderful, and so kind. She was always kind to me. I think I'll go work in the shop and learn the trade. She has two daughters. They're both younger than me. One is just a baby."

Among all my married sisters whom I've placed throughout cities across the United States, my Salt Lake sister remains my favorite. She feels completely real to me as well. Whenever I speak about her, I can picture her clearly, along with her two young daughters and her plumber husband. She's a large, nurturing woman who's just beginning to develop that generous roundness—you know the type, someone who always prepares delicious meals and never loses her temper. She has dark hair. Her husband is a calm, laid-back man. Sometimes I feel like I know him quite intimately. And who's to say I won't encounter him someday? If that elderly sailor could recall Billy Harper, I don't see any reason why I shouldn't eventually meet the husband of my sister who resides in Salt Lake City.

On the other hand, I feel certain that I will never meet my many parents and grandparents in person—you see, I consistently killed them off. Heart disease was my preferred method for eliminating my mother, though sometimes I disposed of her through tuberculosis, pneumonia, and typhoid fever. It's true, as the Winnipeg police officers can confirm, that I have grandparents living in England; but that was a long time ago and it's reasonable to assume they are dead by now. In any case, they have never written to me.

I hope that woman in Reno will read these words and forgive my lack of grace and dishonesty. I'm not apologizing, because I feel no shame. It was my youth, my joy in living, and my eagerness for new experiences that led me to her doorstep. The experience was good for me. It showed me the natural kindness that exists in people. I hope it was good for her too. At least she might get a good laugh out of it now that she discovers what was really going on behind the scenes.

To her, my story was "true." She believed in me and my entire family, and she was deeply concerned about the dangerous journey I would have to make before reaching Salt Lake City. This concern nearly caused me serious trouble. Just as I was about to leave, my arms loaded with lunch and my pockets stuffed with thick woolen socks, she remembered a nephew, or uncle, or some kind of relative, who worked in the railway mail service and who would be coming through that very night on the exact train I planned to sneak a ride on. Perfect! She would take me down to the train station, tell him my story, and convince him to hide me in the mail car. This way, without any danger or hardship, I would be transported directly to Ogden. Salt Lake City was only a few miles beyond that. My heart dropped. She became increasingly excited as she worked out the details of this plan, and with my sinking heart, I had to pretend to feel tremendous joy and excitement about this solution to my problems.

Solution! Why I was headed west that night, and here I was getting trapped into traveling east. It was a trap, and I didn't have the heart to tell her that it was all a terrible lie. And while I pretended that I was thrilled, I was frantically racking my brain for some way to get out of this situation. But there was no escape. She would personally see me into the mail car—she had said so herself—and then that mail-clerk relative of hers would take me to Ogden. And then I would have to make my way back across all those hundreds of miles of desert.

But luck was on my side that evening. Right when she was about to put on her hat and come with me, she realized she had made an error. Her relative who worked as a mail clerk wasn't supposed to pass through that night after all. His route had been modified. He wouldn't be coming through for another two days. I was rescued, because naturally my restless youth wouldn't allow me to wait that long. I confidently told her that I'd reach Salt Lake City faster if I left right away, and I set off with her good wishes and blessings echoing in my ears.

But those wool socks were amazing. I know this for certain. I wore a pair of them that night while riding the blind baggage of the overland train, and that overland train was heading west.

Holding Her Down

Barring accidents, a skilled hobo with youth and agility can stay on a train despite all attempts by the train crew to throw him off—provided, naturally, that it's nighttime, which is an essential requirement. When this type of hobo, under these circumstances, decides he's going to stay on that train, he either succeeds in staying on, or bad luck brings him down. There's no legal method, except for killing him, that allows the train crew to remove him from the train. The belief that train crews haven't hesitated to commit murder is commonly held in the vagrant community. Since I never experienced that specific situation during my own days as a tramp, I can't personally confirm whether it's true.

But this is what I've learned about the "bad" roads. When a hobo has "gone underneath," riding on the rods, and the train is moving, there seems to be no way to remove him until the train comes to a stop. The hobo, comfortably hidden inside the car, surrounded by the four wheels and all the framework, has the upper hand over the crew—or so he believes, until one day he rides the rods on a bad road. A bad road is typically one where a short time before, one or more railroad workers have been killed by hobos. God help the hobo who gets caught "underneath" on such a road—because caught he will be, even if the train is traveling sixty miles per hour.

The "shack" (brakeman) brings a coupling-pin and a section of bell-cord to the platform at the front of the car where the tramp is traveling. The shack attaches the coupling-pin to the bell-cord, lowers it down between the platforms, and feeds out the cord. The coupling-pin hits the railroad ties between the rails, bounces off the bottom of the car, and strikes the ties again. The shack moves it back and forth, first to one side, then to the other, letting it out a little and pulling it in a little, giving his weapon the chance for every kind of impact and bounce. Each strike of that swinging coupling-pin carries death with it, and at sixty miles per hour it pounds out a true rhythm of death. The following day the remains of that tramp are collected along the railroad right-of-way, and a brief notice in the local newspaper mentions the unidentified man, certainly a tramp, probably drunk, who had likely fallen asleep on the tracks.

As a perfect example of how a skilled hobo can manage the situation, I want to share the following experience. I was in Ottawa, heading west on the Canadian Pacific Railway. Three thousand miles of that railroad stretched ahead of me; it was autumn, and I had to cross Manitoba and the Rocky Mountains. I could anticipate harsh weather, and every moment of delay would increase the bitter hardships of the journey. Moreover, I was frustrated. The distance between Montreal and Ottawa is one hundred and twenty miles. I should know, because I had just traveled it and it had taken me six days. By error I had missed the main railway line and traveled on a small branch line with only two local trains a day running on it. And during those six days I had survived on dry bread crusts, and not enough of them, begged from the French farmers.

Furthermore, my disgust had been intensified by the single day I had spent in Ottawa attempting to obtain clothing for my lengthy journey. Let me state for the record right here that Ottawa, with one exception, is the most difficult city in the United States and Canada to beg for clothes in; the one exception is Washington, D.C. That particular city is absolutely the worst. I spent two weeks there trying to beg for a pair of shoes, and then had to continue on to Jersey City before I finally got them.

But to return to Ottawa. At exactly eight in the morning I set out to find clothes. I worked with determination all day long. I swear I walked forty miles. I spoke with the housewives of a thousand homes. I didn't even stop working for dinner. And at six in the afternoon, after ten hours of continuous and discouraging work, I was still missing one shirt, while the pair of pants I had managed to get was tight and, what's more, was showing all the signs that it would fall apart soon.

At six o'clock I finished work and walked toward the railroad yards, planning to find something to eat along the way. But my streak of bad luck continued. House after house turned me away when I asked for food. Then someone gave me a "hand-out." My mood lifted instantly, because it was the biggest hand-out I had ever received in all my long and diverse experience. It was a package wrapped in newspaper, as large as a full-sized suitcase. I rushed to an empty lot and unwrapped it. First, I discovered cake, then more cake, every type and variety of cake imaginable, and still more. The entire package contained nothing but cake. There was no bread and butter with thick, solid slices of meat in between— absolutely nothing except cake; and cake was the one thing I despised above all else! In ancient times and distant lands, people sat by the waters of Babylon and wept. And in an empty lot in Canada's proud capital, I also sat down and wept... over an enormous pile of cake. Just as someone gazes upon the face of their dead child, so did I stare at that overwhelming collection of pastries. I suppose I was an ungrateful vagrant, because I refused to enjoy the generosity of the household that had thrown a party the previous night. Apparently the guests hadn't cared for cake either.

That cake represented the turning point in my luck. Nothing could have been worse than that moment, which meant things had to start getting better. And they did improve. At the very next house, I received what's called a "set-down." A "set-down" represents the ultimate joy for someone in my situation. You're brought inside, often given the opportunity to clean up, and then seated at a proper table. Wanderers cherish the chance to sit at a real table with their legs underneath it. The house was spacious and welcoming, surrounded by extensive grounds filled with beautiful trees, and positioned well away from *The Road*. The family had just finished their meal, and I was brought directly into the dining room—an extraordinarily rare occurrence, since any drifter fortunate enough to earn a set-down typically eats in the kitchen. A distinguished, gray-haired Englishman, his dignified wife, and a lovely young French woman engaged me in conversation while I enjoyed my meal.

I wonder if that beautiful young French woman would remember, even now after all this time, how hard she laughed when I said the crude phrase "two-bits." You see, I was trying tactfully to ask them for a small amount of money. That's how the topic of money came up in our conversation. "What?" she asked. "Two-bits," I replied. Her mouth started to quiver as she asked again, "What?" "Two-bits," I repeated. At that point she exploded into laughter. "Could you say that again?" she requested, once she had composed herself. "Two-bits," I said once more. And again she dissolved into waves of uncontrollable, musical laughter. "I'm sorry," she said, "but what... what exactly did you say?" "Two-bits," I answered. "Is there something wrong with that?" "Not as far as I know," she giggled between breaths, "but what does it mean?" I gave her an explanation, though I can't recall now whether I actually got those two-bits from her or not. But I've often wondered since then which one of us was really the unsophisticated one.

When I got to the train station, I was disgusted to find a group of at least twenty homeless drifters waiting to catch a free ride by hiding in the spaces between train cars on the cross-country route. Two or three people sneaking rides this way is manageable since they can stay hidden. But twenty of them! That was asking for trouble. No train crew would ever allow all of us to ride.

I should explain what a blind baggage is at this point. Some mail cars are constructed without doors at the ends, which makes such a car "blind." The mail cars that do have end doors keep those doors locked at all times. Imagine that after the train has departed, a tramp climbs onto the platform of one of these blind cars. There's no door available, or the door is locked shut. No conductor or brakeman can reach him to collect his fare or remove him from the train. It's obvious that the tramp remains safe until the train makes its next stop. At that point, he has to get off, run forward through the darkness, and when the train passes by, leap back onto the blind car again. However, there are different methods and techniques, as you'll discover.

When the train departed, those twenty hobos rushed toward the three blind baggage cars. Some managed to climb aboard before the train had traveled even one car-length. They were clumsy amateurs, and I could see they would quickly meet their downfall. Naturally, the train crew was aware of what was happening, and at the first stop the problems started. I leaped off and ran forward along the tracks. I observed that several of the hobos were running alongside me. They clearly understood what they were doing. When someone is riding the rails cross-country, they must always stay well ahead of the train during stops. I ran forward, and as I continued running, one by one those who had been keeping pace with me fell behind. This falling behind revealed how skilled and brave each person was at jumping onto a moving train.

Here's how the process works. When the train begins moving, the conductor rides on the blind end of the car. He has no way to return to the main part of the train except by jumping off the blind section and grabbing onto a platform where the car ends aren't blocked from view. When the train reaches a speed that the conductor feels comfortable risking, he jumps off the blind end, allows several cars to pass by, and then boards the train again.

Therefore, it's the hobo's responsibility to run far enough ahead so that by the time the blind section reaches his position, the conductor will have already left it.

I left the last hobo behind by about fifty feet and waited. The train began to move. I could see the brakeman's lantern on the first blind car. He was riding it out. And I watched the inexperienced men stand helplessly by the tracks as the blind car passed them by. They didn't even try to get on. Their own lack of skill had defeated them right from the beginning. Behind them in the lineup came the hobos who knew something about how this worked. They let the first blind car, with the brakeman on it, pass by, and jumped onto the second and third blind cars. Naturally, the brakeman jumped off the first car and onto the second as it rolled past, then scrambled around there, throwing off the men who had climbed aboard. But the important thing was that I had gotten so far ahead that when the first blind car reached me, the brakeman had already left it and was busy dealing with the hobos on the second blind car. A half dozen of the more experienced hobos, who had run far enough forward, also made it onto the first blind car.

At the next stop, as we ran forward along the track, I counted only fifteen of us. Five had been left behind. The elimination process had begun in earnest, and it continued station by station. Now we were fourteen, now twelve, now eleven, now nine, now eight. It reminded me of the ten little Indians from the children's rhyme. I was determined that I should be the last one standing. And why not? Wasn't I blessed with strength, agility, and youth? (I was eighteen, and in perfect condition.) And didn't I have my courage with me? And furthermore, wasn't I a seasoned hobo? Weren't these other vagrants mere novices and inexperienced wanderers compared to me? If I weren't the last one remaining, I might as well abandon this life and find work on an alfalfa farm somewhere.

By the time only four of us were left, the entire train crew had taken notice. From that point forward, it became a battle of skill and intelligence, with the advantage clearly on the crew's side. One after another, the three remaining survivors disappeared, leaving me as the sole holdout. How proud I felt of myself! No wealthy king was ever more satisfied with his first fortune. I was managing to stay on despite the efforts of two brakemen, a conductor, a fireman, and an engineer working against me.

And here are a few examples of how I kept ahead of her. Up ahead in the darkness—so far ahead that the railroad worker riding on the blind baggage car would have to get off before reaching me—I climb on. Good. I'm set for another station. When that station arrives, I dash ahead again to repeat the same move. The train pulls out. I watch her approaching. There's no lantern light on the blind car. Has the crew given up the chase? I don't know. You never know, and you have to be ready for anything at any moment. As the first blind car comes alongside me, and I run to jump aboard, I peer through the darkness to see if the railroad worker is on the platform. For all I know he might be there with his lantern turned off, and just as I leap onto the steps that lantern could come crashing down on my head. I should know better. I've been struck by lanterns two or three times.

But no, the first blind is empty. The train is picking up speed. I'm safe for another station. But am I? I feel the train slow down. Instantly I'm on high alert. Some kind of move is being made against me, and I have no idea what it is. I try to watch both sides at the same time, while making sure to keep an eye on the tender ahead of me. From any one, or all three, of these directions, I might be attacked.

Ah, there it is. The brakeman has made it past the engine. My first warning comes when his feet hit the steps on the right side of the freight car. Like lightning, I jump off the car to the left and run ahead past the engine. I disappear into the darkness. The situation remains the same as it has been ever since the train departed Ottawa. I'm positioned ahead, and the train has to pass by me if it wants to continue its journey. I have just as good an opportunity as before to climb aboard.

I observe closely. I notice a lantern moving toward the engine, but I don't see it return from the engine. It must still be on the engine, and it's reasonable to assume that a railroad worker is holding that lantern. That worker was careless, or he would have extinguished his lantern rather than attempting to cover it as he approached. The train departs. The first freight car's front platform is unoccupied, and I climb aboard it. Just as before when the train slows down, the railroad worker from the engine climbs onto the platform from one side, while I jump off the other side and run toward the front.

As I wait in the darkness, I feel a surge of pride. The transcontinental train has stopped twice for me—for me, just a poor homeless wanderer. I alone have twice stopped the transcontinental express with all its passengers and cars, its government mail, and its two thousand horsepower engine straining ahead. And I weigh only one hundred and sixty pounds, and I don't have a nickel to my name!

Once again, I watch the lantern move toward the front of the train. This time, however, it approaches in a way that's far too obvious. It's much too noticeable for my comfort, and I start wondering what's going on. Regardless, I now have something else to worry about besides the railroad detective on the engine. The train starts moving past me. Just before I'm about to make my jump, I spot the dark silhouette of a railroad detective without a lantern on the first blind baggage car. I let that car pass by and get ready to climb onto the second blind. However, the detective from the first blind has already jumped down and is chasing after me. I also catch a quick glimpse of the lantern belonging to the detective who had been riding on the engine. He has jumped off as well, so now both detectives are on the ground on my side of the train. The next instant, the second blind passes by and I manage to get on board. But I don't stay put. I've already worked out my next move. As I dash across the car's platform, I can hear the detective's feet hitting the steps as he climbs aboard behind me. I leap off the opposite side and run forward alongside the moving train. My strategy is to run ahead and board the first blind. It's going to be close, since the train is picking up speed. The detective is also behind me, running in pursuit. I think I'm the faster runner, because I manage to reach the first blind. I stand on the steps and look back at the man chasing me. He's only about ten feet behind and running hard, but now the train has reached roughly the same speed he's running, so relative to my position, he appears to be standing still. I call out encouragement to him and extend my hand toward him, but he responds with a loud curse, gives up the chase, and boards the train several cars back.

The train races forward, and I'm still laughing to myself when, out of nowhere, a stream of water hits me. The fireman is spraying me with the hose from the engine. I move forward from the car platform to the back of the tender, where I find shelter beneath the overhang. The water shoots harmlessly above my head. My hands are itching to climb up onto the tender and hit that fireman with a piece of coal, but I know that if I do that, both he and the engineer will beat me to a pulp, so I hold back.

At the next stop I get off and move ahead into the darkness. This time, when the train starts moving, both railroad workers are positioned on the first blind car. I can sense what they're planning. They've prevented me from repeating my earlier strategy. I can't take the second blind car again, cross over, and run forward to the first one. As soon as the first blind car passes and I don't climb aboard, they jump off, one on each side of the train. I climb onto the second blind car, and as I do, I realize that in just a moment, at the same time, those two railroad workers will reach me from both sides. It's like being caught in a trap. Both escape routes are cut off. However, there's still another way out, and that way leads upward.

I don't wait for my pursuers to catch up. I climb onto the upright metal framework of the platform and position myself on the hand-brake wheel. This uses up my moment of opportunity, and I hear the railroad workers hitting the steps on both sides. I don't pause to look around. I stretch my arms above my head until my hands touch the downward-curving edges of the two train car roofs. One hand grips the curved roof of one car while the other hand grips the curved roof of the adjacent car. By now both railroad workers are climbing the steps. I'm aware of this, though I'm too focused to actually see them. All of this happens within just a few seconds. I push off with my legs and pull myself up using my arm strength. As I lift my legs up, both railroad workers reach for me but grab nothing but air. I know this because I glance down and see them. I also hear them cursing.

I find myself in a dangerous situation, balancing on the curved edges of two train car roofs simultaneously. With a swift, careful motion, I move both legs onto the curved section of one roof while gripping the curved edge of the other roof with both hands. Then, holding tight to that curved roof edge, I pull myself up and over the curve to reach the flat roof above, where I sit down to rest and catch my breath, keeping a firm grip on a ventilator that sticks up from the surface. I'm now on top of the train—on what hobos call the "decks," and this entire process I've just described is what they refer to as "decking her." I should mention right now that only a young and strong hobo can successfully deck a passenger train, and furthermore, that young and strong hobo must also have steady nerves and courage.

The train continues to pick up speed, and I realize I'm secure until we reach the next station—but only until then. If I stay on the roof after the train comes to a halt, I'm certain those railroad workers will pelt me with stones. A strong worker can drop a fairly heavy piece of rock onto a train car—anywhere from five to twenty pounds. However, there's a good chance that at the next station the workers will be positioned where I originally climbed up, waiting for me to come down. I need to climb down at a different platform instead.

Hoping desperately that there are no tunnels in the next half mile, I stand up and walk down the train about six cars. Let me tell you that you have to leave any fear behind when you take a walk like this. The roofs of passenger cars weren't designed for midnight strolls. If anyone thinks they were, I'd suggest they give it a try. Just have them walk along the roof of a shaking, swaying car with nothing to grab onto except the dark, empty air, and when they reach the curved end of the roof, all wet and slippery from dew, have them speed up to step across to the next roof, which is also curved and wet and slippery. Trust me, they'll quickly discover whether their heart is weak or their head gets dizzy.

As the train slows down for a stop, I climb down from the car roof about half a dozen platforms away from where I had knocked her out. The platform is completely empty. When the train comes to a complete stop, I quietly slip down to the ground. Up ahead, between my position and the engine, I can see two moving lanterns. The railroad detectives are searching for me on top of the train cars. I notice that the car I'm standing next to is a "four-wheeler"—meaning it has only four wheels on each truck assembly. (When you're planning to ride underneath on the rods, make sure to stay away from the "six-wheelers"—they're dangerous and lead to disasters.)

I duck under the train and head for the rods, and I can tell you I'm extremely grateful that the train isn't moving. This is my first time going underneath a Canadian Pacific train, and the internal setup is unfamiliar to me. I attempt to crawl over the top of the truck, between the truck and the bottom of the car. However, the space isn't big enough for me to squeeze through. This is something new to me. Back in the United States, I'm used to going underneath on fast-moving trains, grabbing a gunnel and swinging my feet under to the brake-beam, and from there climbing over the top of the truck and down inside the truck to find a seat on the cross-rod.

Groping around with my hands in the dark, I discover there's space between the brake beam and the ground. It's an extremely tight fit. I need to lie completely flat and wiggle my way through. After getting inside the freight car, I settle myself on the rod and wonder what the hobos are thinking happened to me. The train starts moving. They've finally given up on me.

But have they? At the very next stop, I see a lantern being pushed under the train car next to mine at the other end. They're searching the rods looking for me. I need to escape quickly. I crawl on my belly under the brake beam. They spot me and rush toward me, but I crawl on my hands and knees across the rail on the opposite side and get to my feet. Then I take off running toward the front of the train. I run past the engine and hide in the protective darkness. It's the same old situation. I'm ahead of the train, and the train has to pass by me.

The train starts moving. There's a lantern on the first car. I stay hidden and watch the railroad worker pass by. But there's also a lantern on the second car. That worker spots me and shouts to the worker who has already passed on the first car. Both of them jump off. No matter, I'll take the third car and ride on top. But good heavens, there's a lantern on the third car as well. It's the conductor. I let it pass by. At least now I have the entire train crew ahead of me. I turn around and run back in the direction opposite to where the train is heading. I glance over my shoulder. All three lanterns are on the ground and swaying as they chase after me. I run as fast as I can. Half the train has passed by, and it's moving quite quickly, when I jump aboard. I know that the two railroad workers and the conductor will show up like hungry wolves in about two seconds. I leap onto the hand-brake wheel, grab the curved edges of the roof, and pull myself up to the top; while my frustrated pursuers gather on the platform below like dogs that have cornered a cat up a tree, shouting curses at me and saying rude things about my family.

But what does that matter? It's five against one, counting the engineer and fireman, and they have the full authority of the law and the power of a massive corporation backing them up, yet I'm still outmaneuvering them. I'm positioned too far back on the train, so I sprint forward across the coach rooftops until I reach the fifth or sixth car from the locomotive. I carefully look down below. There's a railroad worker standing on that platform. I can tell he's spotted me by the way he quickly ducks inside the car, and I also know he's lurking just inside the doorway, ready to jump out and grab me the moment I climb down. But I pretend I'm unaware of his presence and stay put to let him think his plan is working. Though I can't see him, I know he cracks the door open once to peek up and confirm I'm still there.

The train begins to slow as it approaches a station. I carefully lower my legs, testing the movement. The train comes to a complete stop. My legs remain hanging down. I can hear the door being quietly unlatched. He's positioned and ready for me. Without warning, I leap to my feet and dash forward across the roof. This puts me directly above his head, where he's waiting inside the doorway. The train sits motionless; the night air is still, and I deliberately make as much noise as possible with my footsteps on the metal roofing. I can't be certain, but I believe he's now rushing forward to intercept me when I climb down at the next platform. However, I have no intention of getting off there. At the midpoint of the coach roof, I pivot around, quietly and swiftly retracing my steps back to the platform that both the vagrant and I had just left behind. The area is completely empty. I climb down to the ground on the far side of the train and conceal myself in the shadows. No one has spotted me.

I walk over to the fence at the edge of the right of way and observe what's happening. Well, well! What do I see there? There's a lantern on top of the train, moving from the front toward the back. They assume I haven't gotten off, so they're searching the rooftops for me. Even better than that—on the ground on both sides of the train, moving in sync with the lantern above, are two more lanterns. It's like a rabbit hunt, and I'm the rabbit they're after. When the railroad detective on top forces me out of hiding, the ones on either side will catch me. I roll a cigarette and watch this whole parade pass by. Once they've moved past my position, I'll be safe to make my way to the front of the train. The train starts moving, and I manage to reach the front blind baggage car without any trouble. But before the train picks up full speed, and just as I'm lighting my cigarette, I realize the fireman has climbed over the coal pile to the back of the tender and is staring down at me. Fear rushes through me. From where he's standing, he could crush me like a bug with chunks of coal. But instead, he speaks to me, and I feel relieved when I hear the admiration in his voice.

"You son-of-a-gun," is what he says.

It's a tremendous honor, and I feel as excited as a student does when receiving an award for excellence.

"Listen," I shout up to him, "don't spray that hose on me anymore."

"All right," he answers, and goes back to his work.

I've become friendly with the engineer, but the brakemen are still hunting for me. At the next station, the brakemen check all three front platforms, and just like before, I let them pass and climb onto the middle of the train. The crew is determined now, and the train comes to a halt. The brakemen are going to throw me off or find out why they can't. Three times the powerful transcontinental train stops for me at that station, and each time I slip past the brakemen and reach the car roofs. But it's useless, because they've finally figured out what's happening. I've shown them that they can't keep me off the train. They'll have to try something different.

And they do exactly that. When the train makes its final stop, they come after me at full speed. Now I understand their strategy. They're attempting to chase me down. Initially they drive me back toward the rear of the train. I recognize the danger I'm in. Once I'm forced to the back of the train, it will depart and leave me stranded. I change direction, weave, and pivot, slipping through my pursuers, and reach the front of the train. One railroad worker continues pursuing me. Fine, I'll give him the chase of his lifetime, since I have excellent stamina. I sprint straight ahead down the railroad tracks. It makes no difference. Even if he follows me for ten miles, he'll still need to catch the train, and I can climb aboard at whatever speed he's capable of maintaining.

So I keep running, staying just comfortably ahead of him while straining my eyes through the darkness to spot cattle guards and railroad switches that could trip me up. Unfortunately, I focus too far ahead and stumble over something right at my feet—I don't know what it was, just some small object—and I crash to the ground in a long, clumsy fall. The next instant I'm back on my feet, but the railroad worker has grabbed me by the collar. I don't fight back. I'm focused on catching my breath and evaluating him. He has narrow shoulders, and I've got at least thirty pounds on him. Plus, he's just as exhausted as I am, and if he tries to hit me, I'll show him a thing or two.

But he doesn't try to hit me, and that issue is resolved. Instead, he begins leading me back toward the train, and another potential problem emerges. I notice the lanterns of the conductor and the other worker. We are getting closer to them. It's not for nothing that I've become familiar with the New York police. It's not for nothing that in freight cars, near water tanks, and in jail cells, I've heard brutal stories of violent treatment. What if these three men are planning to rough me up? God knows I've given them enough reason. I think fast. We are getting closer and closer to the other two railroad workers. I focus on my captor's stomach and jaw, planning the right hook and left cross I'll throw at the first sign of trouble.

Nonsense! I know another technique I'd like to use on him, and I almost wish I had done it the moment I was caught. I could hurt him badly, despite his grip on my collar. His fingers are clenched tight, buried deep inside my collar. My coat is buttoned up completely. Have you ever seen a tourniquet? Well, this works like one. All I need to do is duck my head under his arm and start twisting. I have to twist quickly—very quickly. I know the technique; twisting in a violent, jerky motion, ducking my head under his arm with each turn. Before he realizes what's happening, those gripping fingers of his will be trapped. He won't be able to pull them out. It creates powerful leverage. Twenty seconds after I start spinning, blood will be bursting from his fingertips, the delicate tendons will be tearing, and all the muscles and nerves will be crushing and mashing together in an agonizing mess. Try it sometime when someone grabs you by the collar. But be fast— lightning fast. Also, make sure to protect yourself while you're spinning—shield your face with your left arm and your stomach with your right. You see, the other person might try to stop you by punching with his free arm. It would also be smart to spin away from that free arm rather than toward it. A punch that's moving away is never as bad as one that's coming at you.

That railroad worker will never realize how close he came to getting seriously hurt. The only thing that protects him is that roughing me up isn't part of their strategy. When we get close enough, he shouts that he's caught me, and they signal for the train to keep moving. The locomotive goes past us, followed by the three freight cars. After that, the conductor and the other railroad worker climb aboard. But my captor still keeps his grip on me. I understand their scheme now. He plans to hold me here until the back of the train passes by. Then he'll jump on, leaving me stranded behind—abandoned.

The train has already pulled away quickly, with the engineer attempting to compensate for the delay. Additionally, it's an exceptionally long train. It's moving at a brisk pace, and I can tell the brakeman is gauging its velocity with growing concern.

"Do you think you can make it?" I ask innocently.

He lets go of my collar, makes a quick dash, and jumps aboard. Several more cars still need to pass by. He's aware of this and stays on the steps with his head sticking out, keeping an eye on me. At that moment, my next plan becomes clear. I'll aim for the last platform. I know the train is moving fast and picking up speed, but the worst that could happen is I'll tumble in the dirt if I miss, and I have the confidence that comes with being young. I don't reveal my intentions. I stand there with my shoulders slumped in defeat, making it look like I've given up completely. But at the same time, I'm testing the gravel beneath my feet with my boots. The footing is excellent. I'm also keeping watch on the railroad worker's head poking out. I see him pull it back inside. He's convinced the train is moving too quickly for me to ever catch it.

And the train is moving fast—faster than any train I've ever attempted to board. As the final car passes by, I run alongside it in the same direction. It's a quick, brief sprint. I can't possibly match the train's speed, but I can minimize the difference between our speeds and therefore lessen the impact when I jump aboard. In that brief moment of darkness, I can't see the metal handrail on the rear platform, and there's no time to find it. I reach for where I believe it should be, and at that same instant my feet leave the ground. Everything depends on this moment. The next second I might be tumbling in the gravel with broken ribs, arms, or skull. But my fingers catch hold of the grip, there's a sharp pull on my arms that turns my body slightly, and my feet hit the steps with jarring force.

I sit down, feeling extremely proud of myself. In all my time as a hobo, this is the best train-jumping I've ever accomplished. I understand that late at night you can usually ride several stations on the back platform, but I don't want to risk staying at the rear of the train. At the first stop, I run forward along the side of the train away from the platform, pass the Pullman cars, and crouch down to grab a rod underneath a regular passenger car. At the next stop, I run forward once more and grab another rod.

I am now relatively safe. The railroad workers think I've been thrown off the train. But the long day and the exhausting night are starting to wear me down. Also, it's not as windy or cold underneath, and I begin to drift off. This won't work at all. Falling asleep on the rods means death, so I crawl out at a station and move forward to the second blind. Here I can lie down and sleep; and here I do sleep—I don't know for how long—because I'm awakened by a lantern shoved into my face. The two railroad workers are staring at me. I scramble up defensively, wondering which one is going to take the first swing at me. But fighting is far from their minds.

"I thought you had been ditched," says the guy who had grabbed me by the collar.

"If you hadn't released me when you did, you would have been abandoned along with me," I respond.

"How's that?" he asks.

"I would have gotten into a fight with you, that's all," is my response.

They hold a consultation, and their verdict is summarized as:—

"Well, I suppose you know how to ride, Bo. There's no point in trying to stop you."

39

And they leave and let me stay in peace until their division ends.

I've provided the example above to show what "holding her down" really means. Naturally, I've chosen a successful night from my experiences and haven't mentioned the nights—and there were many of them—when I was caught off guard by chance and ended up crashing.

In conclusion, I want to share what occurred when I arrived at the end of the division. On single-track, cross-country railway lines, freight trains wait at the divisions and depart after the passenger trains have passed through. When I reached the division, I got off my train and searched for the freight train that would leave after it. I located the freight train, assembled on a side track and waiting. I climbed into a boxcar that was half filled with coal and lay down. Within moments I was asleep.

I was woken up by the sound of the door sliding open. Dawn was just breaking, cold and gray, and the freight train hadn't started moving yet. A conductor was sticking his head through the doorway.

"Get out of here, you damn fool!" he shouted at me.

I got off, and outside I watched him walk down the line checking every car on the train. When he disappeared from view I thought to myself that he would never imagine I'd have the courage to climb back into the exact same car from which he had kicked me out. So I climbed back in and lay down again.

Now that criminal's thought process must have been running along the same lines as mine, because he figured out that this was exactly what I would do. So he came back and forced me out.

Now, I was certain he would never imagine I'd try it a third time. I headed back to the exact same train car. But this time I decided to be more careful. Only one side door could be opened. The other side door was boarded shut. Starting from the top of the coal pile, I dug a hole next to that sealed door and lay down inside it. I heard the other door open. The railroad worker climbed up and peered over the top of the coal. He couldn't spot me. He shouted for me to come out. I tried to trick him by staying completely silent. But when he started throwing chunks of coal into the hole on top of me, I surrendered and was kicked out for the third time. He also told me in very strong language what would happen to me if he found me in there again.

I changed my approach. When someone is following your thought patterns, lose them. Suddenly abandon your current reasoning and switch to something completely different. That's exactly what I did. I hid between some cars on a nearby side track and kept watch. Just as I expected, that railroad detective came back to the car again. He opened the door, climbed up, called out, and threw coal into the hole I had created. He even crawled across the coal and peered into the hole. That convinced him I was gone. Five minutes later the freight train was pulling away, and he was nowhere to be seen. I ran alongside the car, yanked the door open, and climbed inside. He never searched for me again, and I rode that coal car for exactly one thousand and twenty-two miles, sleeping most of the journey and getting off at division points (where freight trains always stop for an hour or so) to ask for food. And at the end of those one thousand and twenty-two miles I lost that car because of a fortunate event. I got a "set-down," and there isn't a tramp alive who wouldn't miss a train for a set-down any day.

Pictures

"What does it matter where or how we die,"

   "As long as we have our health to watch it all?"

   —Sestina of the Tramp-Royal

Perhaps the greatest appeal of wandering life is the lack of routine. In the world of drifters, life constantly changes—a continuously shifting spectacle where impossible things occur and surprises emerge from nowhere at every bend in the path. The wanderer never knows what will happen next; therefore, he exists only in the current moment. He has discovered the pointlessness of goal-oriented effort, and understands the joy of moving along with the unpredictable whims of fate.

Often I think about my days as a wanderer, and I'm always amazed by the rapid sequence of images that flash through my memory. It doesn't matter where I start thinking; any single day from all those days stands out on its own, with its own collection of fast-moving scenes. For example, I recall a bright summer morning in Harrisburg, Pennsylvania, and instantly the promising start of that day comes to mind—a proper meal with two unmarried women, and not in their kitchen, but in their dining room, with them sitting beside me at the table. We ate eggs from egg-cups! It was the first time I had ever seen egg-cups, or even heard of egg-cups! I was a little clumsy at first, I'll admit; but I was hungry and unashamed. I figured out the egg-cup, and I conquered those eggs in a way that made those two unmarried women take notice.

They ate like a pair of canaries, picking at the single egg each had taken and nibbling on thin slices of toast. Their bodies held little vitality; their blood flowed weakly; and they had slept in warmth throughout the night. I had spent the entire night outdoors, burning much of my body's energy to stay warm, making my way down from a town called Emporium in the northern region of the state. Thin slices of toast! Unbelievable! But each slice was nothing more than a single mouthful for me—actually, barely even a bite. It becomes tiresome having to reach for another piece of toast with every bite when you're capable of taking many bites.

When I was a very young boy, I had a very small dog named Punch. I took care of feeding him myself. Someone in our household had shot several ducks, and we enjoyed a wonderful meat dinner. After I finished eating, I prepared Punch's meal—a large plate full of bones and scraps. I went outside to give it to him. It so happened that a visitor had ridden over from a nearby ranch, and he had brought with him a Newfoundland dog as large as a calf. I placed the plate on the ground. Punch wagged his tail and started eating. He had at least a delightful half-hour ahead of him. There was a sudden charge. Punch was knocked aside like a piece of straw in a tornado's path, and that Newfoundland dove down onto the plate. Despite his enormous mouth, he must have been trained to eat quickly, because in the brief moment before he got the kick in the ribs that I delivered to him, he completely devoured everything on the plate. He cleaned it entirely. One final lingering swipe of his tongue even removed the grease marks.

As that large Newfoundland dog acted around my dog Punch's food dish, that's exactly how I behaved at the dining table of those two unmarried women from Harrisburg. I cleared everything off it. I didn't damage anything, but I finished all the eggs, toast, and coffee. The maid brought additional servings, but I kept her constantly occupied, and she continued bringing more and more food. The coffee tasted wonderful, but there was no need to serve it in such small cups. How could I find time to eat when it required all my attention to prepare the numerous cups of coffee for drinking?

At any rate, it gave me time to talk. Those two unmarried women, with their rosy-white skin and gray curls, had never experienced the exciting face of adventure. As the "Tramp-Royal" would put it, they had worked their entire lives "on one same shift." Into the pleasant fragrances and limited boundaries of their quiet existence I brought the vast atmosphere of the world, filled with the robust smells of sweat and struggle, and with the sharp scents and aromas of foreign lands and earth. And I deliberately rubbed their soft palms with the calluses on my own hands—the thick, hardened skin that develops from pulling and hauling rope and long, demanding hours of gripping shovel handles. I did this not simply out of youthful boasting, but to demonstrate, through work accomplished, the right I had to their kindness.

Ah, I can picture them now, those wonderful, gentle women, exactly as I sat at their breakfast table twelve years ago, talking about my journey through life, dismissing their caring advice as any true rogue would, and captivating them not only with my own experiences, but with the experiences of all the other men I had met and shared stories with. I claimed all of those adventures as my own—the other men's experiences, that is—and if those unmarried women had been less trusting and innocent, they could have caught me in my contradictory timeline quite easily. But so what? It was a fair trade. In exchange for their many cups of coffee, eggs, and pieces of toast, I provided excellent value. I gave them magnificent entertainment. My presence at their table was their adventure, and adventure is priceless regardless.

Walking down the street after saying goodbye to the elderly women, I picked up a newspaper from someone's doorstep—clearly left by a late sleeper—and found a grassy spot in a nearby park to catch up on what had happened in the world over the past day. While I was there in the park, I encountered another homeless wanderer who shared his life story with me and tried hard to convince me to enlist in the United States Army. He had already given in to a military recruiter and was about to sign up, and he couldn't understand why I wouldn't join alongside him. He had been part of Coxey's Army during their march to Washington a few months earlier, and that experience seemed to have sparked his interest in military service. I was also a veteran of sorts, having served as a private in Company L of the Second Division of Kelly's Industrial Army—a unit that everyone called the "Nevada push." However, my time with that army had affected me in completely the opposite way; so I left that fellow vagrant to pursue his path toward the machinery of war, while I went off to find myself some dinner.

After completing this duty, I began walking across the bridge over the Susquehanna toward the west shore. I can't recall the name of the railroad that ran along that side, but while lying in the grass that morning, the idea had occurred to me to travel to Baltimore; so I was heading to Baltimore on that railroad, regardless of what it was called. The afternoon was warm, and halfway across the bridge I encountered a group of men who were swimming near one of the piers. I quickly removed my clothes and jumped in. The water felt wonderful; however, when I emerged and got dressed, I discovered I had been robbed. Someone had searched through my clothing. Now I ask you, isn't being robbed adventure enough for a single day? I have known people who were robbed and spent the remainder of their lives talking about the experience. Admittedly, the thief who rifled through my clothes didn't obtain much—perhaps thirty or forty cents in nickels and pennies, along with my tobacco and cigarette papers; but it represented everything I owned, which is more than most people can lose to robbery, since they typically have possessions remaining at home, whereas I had no home. It was quite a rough crowd swimming there. I assessed the situation and knew better than to complain. So I asked for "the makings," and I could have sworn it was one of my own papers that I used to roll the tobacco.

Then I hiked across the bridge to the western shore. The railroad I was looking for ran through this area. I couldn't see any station nearby. The challenge was figuring out how to catch a freight train without having to walk all the way to a station. I observed that the tracks climbed up a steep incline, reaching their highest point right where I had encountered them, and I realized that a heavy freight train wouldn't be able to move very quickly up such a grade. But exactly how slow would it go? On the far side of the tracks, there was a tall embankment. At the top edge, I spotted a man's head poking up above the grass. He might know how fast the freight trains usually took this grade, and when the next southbound train was due. I shouted my questions up to him, and he gestured for me to climb up and join him.

I followed his instructions, and when I reached the summit, I discovered four other men resting in the grass alongside him. I surveyed the scene and recognized them for what they were— American gypsies. In the clearing that stretched back through the trees from the riverbank's edge stood several worn, unremarkable wagons. Tattered, barely clothed children ran throughout the camp, though I observed that they were careful not to approach or disturb the men. Several thin, unattractive, and work-worn women busied themselves with camp duties, and I noticed one who sat alone on the seat of one of the wagons, her head hanging forward, her knees pulled up to her chin and held loosely by her arms. She didn't appear happy. She looked as though she cared about nothing—in this I was mistaken, for later I would discover that there was indeed something she cared deeply about. The complete extent of human anguish was written across her face, and beyond that, there was the tragic look of someone unable to endure any more pain. Her expression seemed to convey that nothing could cause her further harm; but in this assessment, too, I was wrong.

I lay in the grass at the edge of the steep slope and talked with the men. We were family—brothers. I was the American hobo, and they were the American gypsy. I understood enough of their slang to have a conversation, and they understood enough of mine. There were two others in their group who were across the river "mushing" in Harrisburg. A "musher" is a traveling con artist. This word shouldn't be confused with the Klondike "musher," though both terms might have the same origin; specifically, the corruption of the French marche ons, meaning to march, to walk, to "mush." The specific scam of the two mushers who had crossed the river was umbrella repair; but what real scheme lay behind their umbrella repair work, I wasn't told, nor would it have been proper to ask.

It was a beautiful day. There wasn't even the slightest breeze, and we enjoyed the sparkling warmth of the sunshine. The sleepy buzzing of insects could be heard from all directions, and the mild air was rich with the fragrances of fertile soil and flourishing plants. We felt too relaxed to do anything more than speak in occasional, quiet exchanges. Then, suddenly, the tranquility and calm was disrupted by human presence.

Two boys around eight or nine years old, both barefoot, somehow broke one of the camp's rules—I couldn't tell what they had done. A man lying next to me suddenly sat up and shouted at them. He was the tribe's leader, a man with a narrow forehead and eyes that were mere slits, whose thin lips and twisted, mocking expression made it clear why both boys flinched and went rigid like frightened deer when they heard his voice. Fear showed sharp and alert in their faces, and they spun around, ready to bolt in panic. He yelled for them to come back, and one boy hung back hesitantly, his small, skinny body acting out the battle raging inside him between terror and logic. He wanted to return. His mind and everything he'd learned before told him that coming back would be the better choice than running away; but even though it was the lesser of two evils, it was still terrible enough to fuel his fear and make his feet itch to run.

Still he stumbled and fought his way forward until he made it to the safety of the trees, where he stopped. The tribal leader chose not to follow him. Instead, he walked casually to a wagon and grabbed a heavy whip. Then he returned to the middle of the clearing and stood motionless. He said nothing. He made no hand movements. He embodied the Law itself, merciless and all-powerful. He simply remained there and waited. And I understood, and everyone understood, and the two boys hiding among the trees understood, exactly what he was waiting for.

The boy who had fallen behind slowly returned. His face showed trembling determination. He didn't hesitate. He had decided to accept his punishment. And notice this: the punishment wasn't for his original wrongdoing, but for the crime of running away. In doing this, that tribal leader was simply acting the same way as the civilized society he belonged to. We punish our criminals, and when they escape and flee, we capture them and increase their punishment.

The boy walked directly to the chief, stopping at just the right distance for the whip to reach him. The lash whistled through the air, and I found myself startled by how hard the strike was. The child's thin little leg looked so fragile and small. The skin turned white where the whip had wrapped around and cut in, and then, where it had been white, an angry red welt rose up, with small drops of blood seeping out here and there where the skin had split open. The whip came down again, and the boy's entire body flinched as he braced for the strike, though he didn't move from his position. His determination held strong. A second welt appeared, then a third. It wasn't until the fourth blow hit that the boy cried out. He also couldn't stay still anymore, and from that point on, with each strike that followed, he jumped up and down in pain, screaming; but he didn't try to run away. When his uncontrollable movements carried him out of the whip's reach, he moved back within range again. And when it was finished—twelve strikes in total—he walked away, whimpering and crying, toward the wagons.

The chief remained motionless and waited. The second boy emerged from the trees. However, he didn't approach directly. He moved like a cowering dog, gripped by sudden bursts of fear that caused him to spin around and dash away for several steps. Yet he always turned back and returned, moving in circles that brought him closer and closer to the man, whimpering and making wordless animal sounds in his throat. I noticed that he never looked at the man. His gaze stayed locked on the whip, and in his eyes was a terror that made me feel sick—the desperate fear of a child who had been unimaginably abused. I have watched strong men falling left and right in battle and writhing in their final moments, I have seen them blown into the air by the dozens from exploding shells with their bodies ripped apart; trust me, witnessing those scenes was like celebration and joy and music to me compared to how the sight of that suffering child affected me.

The beating started. The whipping of the first boy seemed like child's play compared to this one. Blood quickly began streaming down his skinny little legs. He twisted and writhed and curled up until he looked almost like some bizarre puppet controlled by strings. I say "looked," because his screaming revealed the truth behind the appearance and marked it with harsh reality. His cries were sharp and piercing; there were no rough tones in them, only the thin, genderless quality of a child's voice. The moment arrived when the boy couldn't endure it any longer. His mind snapped, and he attempted to flee. But the man pursued him, blocking his escape, driving him back with strikes into the open area again and again.

Then came an interruption. I heard a wild, muffled cry. The woman who had been sitting in the wagon seat climbed out and ran over to intervene. She jumped between the man and the boy.

"You want some, eh?" he said, holding the whip. "All right, then."

He struck her with the whip. Since her skirts were long, he didn't aim for her legs. Instead, he directed the lash toward her face, which she protected as well as she could with her hands and forearms, bending her head down between her thin shoulders, taking the blows on her slender shoulders and arms. What a brave mother! She understood exactly what she was doing. The boy, still screaming, was escaping toward the wagons.

And the entire time, the four men lay next to me, watching without making any movement. I didn't move either, and I admit this without any shame, even though my mind had to fight hard against my natural urge to stand up and step in. I understood how life worked. What good would it do the woman, or myself, if I got beaten to death by five men there on the banks of the Susquehanna River? I once witnessed a man being hanged, and although my entire soul screamed in protest, I kept my mouth shut. If I had spoken up, I most likely would have had my skull smashed in by the handle of a gun, because it was the law that this man had to hang. And here, among this gypsy group, it was their law that the woman had to be whipped.

Even so, the reason I didn't intervene in either situation wasn't because it was the law, but because the law was more powerful than I was. If those four men hadn't been lying beside me in the grass, I would have gladly attacked the man with the whip. And unless I had the bad luck of one of the camp women hitting me with a knife or club, I'm confident I would have beaten him to a pulp. But those four men were there beside me in the grass. They made their law stronger than mine.

Oh, believe me, I suffered right along with her. I had witnessed women being beaten before, many times, but I had never seen a beating like this one. Her dress was torn to ribbons across her shoulders. One strike that got past her defense had left a bloody welt running from her cheek down to her chin. Not just one blow, or two, not a dozen or even two dozen, but endlessly, without stopping, that whip lashed out and wrapped around her body. Sweat poured down my face, and I struggled to breathe, gripping the grass with my hands so tightly that I pulled it up by the roots. The entire time, my mind kept telling me, "You fool! You fool!" That welt on her face almost broke me completely. I began to stand up, but the hand of the man beside me reached out to my shoulder and pushed me back down.

"Take it easy, partner, take it easy," he cautioned me quietly. I turned to look at him. His gaze met mine steadily. He was a big man with broad shoulders and thick muscles; his face appeared lazy, sluggish, and lethargic, though there was kindness in it, yet it lacked any real emotion and seemed completely empty—a dull spirit, harmless, without morals, like cattle, and obstinate. He was simply an animal, possessing only the faintest glimmer of intelligence, a good-natured beast with the physical power and mental capacity of a gorilla. His hand weighed down heavily on me, and I could feel the force of the muscles beneath it. I glanced at the other beasts, two of them calm and uninterested, and one who seemed to take pleasure in watching what was happening; then my sanity returned to me, my muscles loosened, and I collapsed into the grass.

My thoughts drifted back to the two unmarried women I had shared breakfast with that morning. Less than two miles away, in a straight line, they were separated from this scene unfolding before me. Here, on this still day beneath a kind sun, one of their sisters was being struck by one of my brothers. This was a slice of life they would never witness—and perhaps that was for the best, though without seeing such things they could never truly understand their connection to other women, nor grasp who they really were, nor comprehend what they were made of. For women cannot live sheltered lives in pleasant, confined spaces while also being a caring sister to everyone in the world.

The beating was over, and the woman, who had stopped screaming, returned to her place in the wagon. The other women didn't go to her right away. They were scared. But they approached her later, after enough time had passed. The man put his whip away and came back to join us, throwing himself down on the other side of me. He was breathing heavily from the effort. He wiped the sweat from his eyes with his coat sleeve and stared at me defiantly. I met his gaze casually; what he had done wasn't my business. I didn't leave suddenly. I stayed there for another half hour, which, given the situation, was the polite and proper thing to do. I rolled cigarettes using tobacco I borrowed from them, and when I slid down the embankment to the railroad tracks, I had all the information I needed to catch the next freight train heading south.

Well, so what? It was just one page from life, nothing more; and I've witnessed many pages that are much worse, far worse than that. I've occasionally argued (jokingly, or so my audience thought) that the main difference between humans and other animals is that humans are the only species that mistreats their own females. This is behavior that no wolf or even a cowardly coyote would ever engage in. This is something that even dogs, weakened by domestication, refuse to do. Dogs still maintain their wild instincts in this regard, while humans have lost most of their natural instincts—at least, most of the good ones.

Worse chapters of life than what I've just described? Read the reports on child labor in the United States—east, west, north, and south, the location doesn't matter—and understand that all of us, driven by profit as we are, create and produce far worse chapters of human suffering than that single incident of domestic violence along the Susquehanna River.

I walked down the slope about a hundred yards to where the ground next to the railroad tracks was solid. This was where I could hop onto my freight train as it slowly climbed the hill, and this was where I discovered half a dozen drifters waiting for the same opportunity. Some of them were playing seven-up with a worn deck of cards. I joined the game. A Black man started shuffling the cards. He was heavy-set, young, and had a round face. He radiated friendliness. It practically flowed out of him. As he dealt the first card to me, he stopped and said:—

"Say, Bo, haven't I seen you before?"

"You certainly have," I replied. "And you weren't wearing those same clothes, either."

He was confused.

"Do you remember Buffalo?" I asked.

Then he recognized me, and with laughter and excited exclamations welcomed me as a fellow companion; because at Buffalo his clothes had been striped while he served his sentence in the Erie County Penitentiary. As it happened, my clothes had been striped in the same way, since I had been serving my time there as well.

The game continued, and I discovered what we were playing for. A steep and narrow trail led down the bank toward the river, descending to a spring about twenty-five feet below. We played our game right at the edge of the bank. Whoever lost had to grab a small condensed-milk can and use it to carry water back up to the winners.

The first game was played and the newcomer lost. He grabbed the small milk tin and climbed down the riverbank while we sat above and made fun of him. We drank enormous amounts. He had to make four round trips just for me, and the others were just as generous with their thirst. The path was extremely steep, and sometimes the newcomer slipped partway up, spilled the water, and had to go back for more. But he didn't lose his temper. He laughed just as hard as any of us; that's why he slipped so frequently. He also promised us he would drink massive quantities of water when someone else got stuck.

When we had satisfied our thirst, we began another round of the game. Once more the man was trapped, and once again we drank until we were completely satisfied. A third and fourth game ended exactly the same way, and each time that round-faced man nearly collapsed with joy at how fortune was treating him. We almost collapsed along with him from our own delight. We laughed like carefree children, or like gods, there on the riverbank's edge. I know I laughed until it felt like the top of my head might pop off, and I drank from the tin cup until I was practically waterlogged. We began seriously discussing whether we could successfully climb aboard the freight train when it came up the slope, considering how much water we had stored in our bodies. This particular aspect of our situation nearly finished off our companion completely. He had to stop carrying water for at least five minutes while he lay down and rolled around laughing.

The growing shadows extended further and further across the river, and the gentle, cool dusk arrived, and still we drank water, and still our dark-skinned cup-bearer brought us more and more. The beaten woman from an hour earlier was forgotten. That was a page read and turned; I was occupied now with this fresh page, and when the train whistle sounded on the slope, this page would be complete and another would start; and that's how the book of life continues, page after page and endless pages—when one is young.

And then we played a game where the newcomer couldn't be caught. The target was a thin and sickly-looking vagrant, the one who had laughed the least among all of us. We said we didn't want any water—which was true. Not all the riches of the East, nor the force of a hydraulic press, could have pushed another drop into my completely saturated body. The newcomer looked disappointed, then rose to meet the challenge and said he'd have some. He was serious about it, too. He had some, and then more, and then even more. Again and again the gloomy vagrant climbed down and up the steep embankment, and again and again the newcomer called for more. He drank more water than all the rest of us combined. The twilight grew darker into night, the stars appeared, and he continued drinking. I truly believe that if the freight train's whistle hadn't blown, he'd still be there, guzzling water and getting his revenge while the gloomy vagrant labored down and up.

But the whistle blew. The page had turned. We jumped to our feet and lined up along the railroad track. There it came, coughing and sputtering as it climbed the slope, its headlight cutting through the darkness and casting our silhouettes in stark detail. The locomotive rolled past us, and we all started running alongside the train, some climbing onto the side ladders while others pried open the side doors of empty freight cars and hauled themselves inside. I grabbed hold of a flatcar carrying various pieces of lumber and crawled into a cozy spot. I stretched out on my back, using a newspaper as a makeshift pillow beneath my head. Overhead, the stars twinkled and seemed to wheel in formations back and forth as the train took the curves, and watching them I drifted off to sleep. The day had ended—just one day among all my days. Tomorrow would bring another day, and I was young.

Stolen

I traveled to Niagara Falls in a "side-door Pullman," or in everyday language, a freight car. A flat-car, incidentally, is called a "gondola" among hobos, with the second syllable stressed and drawn out. But back to my story. I arrived in the afternoon and went directly from the freight train to the falls. Once I saw that magnificent sight of cascading water, I was completely captivated. I couldn't pull myself away long enough to "panhandle" at the "houses" (homes) for my dinner. Even a proper sit-down meal couldn't have drawn me away. Evening arrived, a gorgeous moonlit night, and I stayed by the falls until past eleven o'clock. Then I had to search for a place to sleep.

"Kip," "doss," "flop," "pound your ear," all mean the same thing; namely, to sleep. Somehow, I had a feeling that Niagara Falls was a dangerous town for hoboes, and I headed out into the countryside. I climbed over a fence and lay down to sleep in a field. The police would never find me there, I told myself confidently. I lay on my back in the grass and slept like a baby. It was so pleasantly warm that I didn't wake up once all night. But with the first gray light of dawn my eyes opened, and I remembered the magnificent falls. I climbed over the fence and started down *The Road* to take another look at them. It was early—no more than five o'clock—and not until eight o'clock could I begin to ask for my breakfast. I could spend at least three hours by the river. Unfortunately! I was destined never to see the river or the falls again.

The town was sleeping when I arrived. Walking down the quiet street, I noticed three men approaching me on the sidewalk. They were walking side by side. I figured they were drifters, just like me, who had gotten up early. My guess wasn't entirely right. I was only sixty-six and two-thirds percent accurate. The men on either side were indeed drifters, but the one in the middle wasn't. I moved toward the edge of the sidewalk to let the three of them pass. But they didn't pass by. At a word from the man in the center, all three stopped, and the one in the middle spoke to me.

I understood the situation immediately. He was an undercover police officer and the two hoboes were his prisoners. The law was up early hunting for the early catch. I was that catch. If I had possessed the experience that would come to me over the next several months, I would have turned and run like hell. He might have shot at me, but he would have had to actually hit me to stop me. He never would have chased after me, because two hoboes already captured are worth more than one trying to escape. But like a fool I stood there motionless when he stopped me. Our conversation was short.

"What hotel are you staying at?" he asked.

He had caught me. I wasn't planning to stay at any hotel, and since I didn't know the name of a single hotel in town, I couldn't pretend to be staying at one of them. On top of that, I was out far too early in the morning. Everything was working against me.

"I just arrived," I said.

"Well, you turn around and walk in front of me, and not too far in front. There's somebody wants to see you."

I was arrested. I knew who wanted to see me. With that undercover police officer and the two vagrants following behind me, and under the direction of the officer, I led the way to the city jail. There we were searched and our names were recorded. I have forgotten now which name I was registered under. I gave the name of Jack Drake, but when they searched me, they found letters addressed to Jack London. This caused problems and required an explanation, all of which has faded from my memory, and to this day I do not know whether I was arrested as Jack Drake or Jack

London. But one name or the other should be there today in the prison records of Niagara Falls. Research could bring it to light. The time was somewhere in the latter part of June, 1894. It was only a few days after my arrest that the great railroad strike began.

From the office, we were taken to the "Hobo" and locked inside. The "Hobo" is the section of a prison where minor offenders are held together in a large iron cage. Because hoboes make up the main group of minor offenders, this iron cage is called the Hobo. There we encountered several hoboes who had already been arrested that morning, and every so often the door would be unlocked and two or three more would be pushed in with us. Finally, when our number reached sixteen, we were taken upstairs to the courtroom. And now I will honestly describe what happened in that courtroom, because you should know that my patriotic American citizenship received a shock there from which it has never completely recovered.

In the courtroom sat sixteen prisoners, along with the judge and two bailiffs. The judge appeared to be serving as his own clerk. No witnesses were present. No citizens from Niagara Falls had come to observe how justice was being carried out in their community. The judge looked down at the list of cases in front of him and called out a name. A vagrant stood up. The judge glanced toward a bailiff. "Vagrancy, your Honor," the bailiff announced. "Thirty days," his Honor declared. The vagrant sat back down, and the judge was already calling another name as another vagrant rose to his feet.

The trial of that homeless man had lasted roughly fifteen seconds. The trial of the next homeless man proceeded with the same speed. The bailiff announced, "Vagrancy, your Honor," and his Honor responded, "Thirty days." This continued like clockwork, fifteen seconds per homeless man—and thirty days.

They were like helpless, silent animals, I thought to myself. But just wait until it's my turn; I'll give his Honor quite a speech.

Partway through the proceedings, his Honor, prompted by some impulse, gave one of us a chance to speak. As luck would have it, this man wasn't a real hobo. He didn't have any of the telltale signs of a professional drifter. If he had come up to the rest of us while we were waiting by a water tank for a freight train, we would have immediately labeled him a "gay-cat." Gay-cat is what hobos call a newcomer. This gay-cat was getting on in years—around forty-five, I'd estimate. His shoulders were slightly hunched, and his face was lined and weathered.

For many years, according to his account, he had driven a team for some company in Lockport, New York, if I recall correctly. The company had stopped doing well, and eventually, during the difficult economic times of 1893, it went out of business entirely. He had been kept on until the very end, although toward the final period his work had become quite sporadic. He continued and described in detail his struggles to find employment during the following months, when so many people were unemployed. Eventually, deciding that he would discover better job opportunities around the Lakes, he had set out for Buffalo. Naturally he was completely without money, and there he found himself. That was the whole story.

"Thirty days," the judge announced, then called out another homeless man's name.

The homeless man stood up. "Vagrancy, your Honor," the bailiff announced, and the judge responded, "Thirty days."

And that's how it continued, with each homeless person receiving fifteen seconds of attention and thirty days in jail. The justice system was operating like clockwork. Most likely, given how early it was in the morning, the judge hadn't eaten breakfast yet and was eager to get through the cases quickly.

But my American spirit was fired up. Behind me stood the many generations of my American forebears. One of the freedoms those ancestors of mine had battled and perished for was the right to trial by jury. This was my inheritance, made sacred by their sacrifice, and it fell to me to defend it. Very well, I promised myself; just wait until he gets to me.

He reached me. My name, whatever it was, got called out, and I stood up. The bailiff announced, "Vagrancy, your Honor," and I started to speak. But the judge started talking at the exact same time, and he declared, "Thirty days." I tried to object, but right then his Honor was already calling out the name of the next homeless person on the list. His Honor stopped just long enough to tell me, "Shut up!" The bailiff pushed me back down into my seat. And the very next moment that following homeless person had gotten thirty days and the one after him was already in the middle of receiving his sentence.

When we had all received our sentences of thirty days each, the judge was just about to dismiss us when he suddenly turned to the truck driver from Lockport—the only man he had permitted to speak.

"Why did you quit your job?" his Honor asked.

Now the truck driver had already explained how he had lost his job, and the question caught him off guard.

"Your Honor," he started awkwardly, "isn't that a strange question to ask?"

"Thirty more days to quit your job," the judge declared, and the court session ended. That was the verdict. The truck driver received a total of sixty days, while the rest of us were given thirty days.

We were brought downstairs, locked up, and served breakfast. It was a fairly decent breakfast by prison standards, and it turned out to be the best meal I would receive for the next month.

As for me, I was stunned. There I was, sentenced after a mockery of a trial where I was denied not only my right to a jury trial, but also my right to enter a plea of guilty or not guilty. Another principle my ancestors had fought for flashed through my mind—habeas corpus. I would show them. But when I requested a lawyer, they laughed at me. Habeas corpus was fine in theory, but what good did it do me when I couldn't contact anyone outside the jail? But I would show them. They couldn't hold me in jail indefinitely. Just wait until I got out, that was all. I would make them take notice. I understood something about the law and my own rights, and I would expose their mishandling of justice. Images of lawsuits and shocking newspaper headlines were dancing in my mind when the guards entered and started rushing us out into the main office.

A police officer fastened a handcuff around my right wrist. (Ah, I thought to myself, another humiliation. Just wait until I'm free.) He attached the other handcuff from that pair to the left wrist of a Black man. This man was exceptionally tall, well over six feet— so tall that when we stood next to each other, his hand pulled mine up slightly in the shackles. He was also the most cheerful and most tattered Black man I had ever encountered.

We were all handcuffed in the same way, two people together. Once this was done, they brought out a shiny nickel-steel chain, threaded it through the links of all our handcuffs, and secured it at both the front and back of our double line. We had become a chain gang. The order to march was given, and we stepped out onto the street, watched over by two officers. The tall Black man and I were given the place of honor. We led the procession.

After the tomb-like darkness of the prison, the sunlight outside was blinding. I had never experienced it as so precious as I did now, a prisoner wearing rattling chains, knowing that I would soon lose sight of it for thirty days. We walked through the streets of Niagara Falls toward the train station, watched by curious onlookers, and particularly by a crowd of tourists on the porch of a hotel we passed by.

There was plenty of slack in the chain, and with much rattling and clanking we sat down, two by two, in the seats of the smoking car. Though I was burning with anger at the injustice that had been committed against me and my ancestors, I was still too practically minded to lose control over it. This was all completely new to me. Thirty days of uncertainty lay ahead of me, and I looked around to find someone who understood how things worked. I had already discovered that I wasn't heading to some small jail with around a hundred prisoners, but to a full-scale penitentiary housing a couple thousand inmates, serving sentences ranging from ten days to ten years.

In the seat behind me, chained by his wrist, sat a short, heavily-built man with powerful muscles. He appeared to be somewhere between thirty-five and forty years old. I studied him carefully. In the corners of his eyes, I could see humor, laughter, and kindness. As for everything else about him, he was like a savage animal, completely without morals, filled with all the raw passion and violent intensity of a wild beast. What redeemed him, what made him tolerable to me, were those corners of his eyes—the humor, laughter, and kindness of the beast when it wasn't provoked.

He was my target. I was drawn to him. While my handcuffed companion, the tall Black man, grieved with chuckles and laughter over some laundry he was certain to lose because of his arrest, and while the train continued rolling toward Buffalo, I spoke with the man sitting behind me. He had an empty pipe. I filled it for him with my valuable tobacco—enough in a single filling to make a dozen cigarettes. Indeed, the more we talked the more certain I became that he was my target, and I shared all my tobacco with him.

I happen to be the kind of person who adapts easily, with enough connection to life to blend in almost anywhere. I made an effort to get along with this man, though I had no idea how remarkably well this would serve me. He had never been to the specific prison where we were headed, but he had served one-, two-, and five-year sentences in various other prisons (a "spot" means a year), and he was full of knowledge. We became quite friendly, and my spirits lifted when he warned me to follow his example. He called me "Jack," and I called him "Jack."

The train came to a stop at a station roughly five miles outside Buffalo, and we—the chain gang—stepped off. I can't recall the exact name of this station, but I'm certain it was one of these: Rocklyn, Rockwood, Black Rock, Rockcastle, or Newcastle. Regardless of what the place was called, we walked a short distance before boarding a streetcar. It was an old-style car with a long bench seat running along each side. All the passengers sitting on one side were asked to move to the other side, and we took their spots with a loud clanking of chains. We sat facing them, I recall, and I also remember the frightened looks on the women's faces—they clearly thought we were convicted murderers and bank robbers. I tried to appear as menacing as possible, but my fellow prisoner, that overly cheerful Black man, kept rolling his eyes, laughing, and repeating over and over, "O Lord! Lord!"

We got out of the car, walked a bit further, and were brought into the office of the Erie County Penitentiary. This was where we had to register, and you'll find one of my names or the other on that registration record. We were also told that we had to leave all our valuable items in the office: cash, tobacco, matches, pocket knives, and other similar things.

My new friend shook his head at me.

"If you don't leave your belongings here, they'll be taken away once you go inside," the official warned.

Still my friend shook his head. He was working with his hands, concealing his actions behind the other men. (Our handcuffs had been taken off.) I observed him and did the same, wrapping everything I wanted to bring inside into a bundle using my handkerchief. Both of us stuffed these bundles into our shirts. I saw that our fellow prisoners, except for one or two who owned watches, didn't hand over their possessions to the man at the desk.

They were determined to sneak them in somehow, hoping for the best; but they weren't as clever as my friend, since they didn't wrap their belongings in bundles.

Our former guards collected the handcuffs and chains and left for Niagara Falls, while we, now under new guards, were escorted into the prison. During our time in the office, other groups of newly arrived prisoners had joined us, so we had become a procession of forty or fifty people.

Know, those of you who are free, that movement is as limited inside a large prison as trade was during the Middle Ages. Once you're inside a penitentiary, you can't walk around wherever you want. Every few steps you come across massive steel doors or gates that stay locked at all times. We were heading to the barber shop, but we ran into delays while waiting for doors to be unlocked for us. This held us up in the first "hall" we walked into. A "hall" isn't a hallway. Picture a rectangular box made of bricks that stretches six stories tall, with each floor containing a row of cells—about fifty cells per row—basically, picture a massive cube that looks like a giant honeycomb. Put this cube on the ground and surround it with a building that has a roof on top and walls on every side. This cube and the building around it make up what's called a "hall" in the Erie County Penitentiary. Also, to get the complete picture, imagine a narrow walkway with steel railings that runs along the entire length of each level of cells, and at the ends of this rectangular cube, picture all these walkways from both sides connected by a fire escape system made of narrow steel staircases.

We stopped in the first hall, waiting for a guard to unlock a door. Scattered around the area were prisoners with closely cut hair and clean-shaven faces, dressed in striped prison uniforms. I spotted one particular prisoner above us on the walkway of the third level of cells. He stood on the gallery leaning forward with his arms resting on the rail, seemingly unaware of our presence. He appeared to be staring into empty space. My companion made a quiet hissing sound. The prisoner looked down. Silent signals were exchanged between them. Then my companion's handkerchief bundle flew through the air. The prisoner caught it, and in an instant it disappeared into his shirt while he returned to staring blankly ahead. My companion had instructed me to follow his example. I waited for my opportunity when the guard turned away, and my bundle followed the first one into the prisoner's shirt.

A minute later, the door was unlocked, and we walked single file into the barbershop. Inside, there were more men wearing the striped prison uniforms. These were the prison barbers. The room also contained bathtubs, hot water, soap, and scrubbing brushes. We received orders to undress and wash ourselves, with each man required to scrub his neighbor's back—this mandatory bath was a pointless safety measure, since the prison was crawling with bugs and lice. Following our bath, each of us received a canvas bag for our clothes.

"Put all your clothes in the bags," the guard said. "There's no point trying to sneak anything inside. You need to line up naked for inspection. Men serving thirty days or less can keep their shoes and suspenders. Men serving more than thirty days keep nothing."

This announcement caused widespread alarm. How could naked men possibly smuggle anything past an inspection? Only my friend and I were protected. But this was exactly where the convict barbers did their dirty work. They moved among the unfortunate newcomers, generously offering to look after their precious few possessions, and promising to give them back later that day. Those barbers were charitable souls—if you listened to their words. Just like in the case of Fra Lippo Lippi, there was never such quick relieving of burdens. Matches, tobacco, rolling papers, pipes, knives, money, everything flowed into the roomy shirts of the barbers. They practically bulged with their stolen goods, and the guards pretended not to notice. To make a long story short, nothing was ever given back. The barbers never had any plan to return what they had stolen. They believed it rightfully belonged to them. This was the barber-shop scam. There were many scams in that prison, as I would discover; and I, too, was meant to become a con artist—thanks to my new friend.

The shop contained multiple chairs, and the barbers moved with incredible speed. I witnessed the fastest shaves and haircuts I had ever seen in my life. The customers applied their own lather, while the barbers shaved each man in roughly sixty seconds. A haircut required only slightly more time. Within three minutes, the soft facial hair of my eighteen years had been scraped away, leaving my head as smooth as a billiard ball with just the beginning stubble of new growth. Beards and mustaches disappeared completely, just like our clothing and everything else we had brought with us. Believe me when I say we looked like a gang of criminals by the time they finished with us. Until that moment, I hadn't truly understood just how thoroughly rough and disreputable we appeared.

Then came the lineup, forty or fifty of us, naked like Kipling's heroes who stormed Lungtungpen. Searching us was simple. There were only our shoes and ourselves. Two or three reckless individuals, who had questioned the barbers' advice, were caught with contraband—tobacco, pipes, matches, and small change— which was immediately seized. Once this was finished, our new clothing was brought to us—heavy prison shirts, and jackets and pants with bold stripes. I had always believed that convict stripes were only put on a person after they had been found guilty of a serious crime. I no longer held that belief, but put on the symbols of disgrace and experienced my first taste of marching in lockstep.

Walking in single file, pressed close together with each man's hands resting on the shoulders of the person ahead, we continued marching into another spacious hall. There we were lined up against the wall in a lengthy row and commanded to bare our left arms. A young man, a medical student who was practicing his skills on livestock like us, moved down the line. He administered vaccinations roughly four times faster than the barbers had shaved us. With a final warning not to rub our arms against anything and to allow the blood to dry so it would form a scab, we were escorted to our cells. This is where my companion and I separated, though not before he managed to whisper to me, "Suck it out."

As soon as they locked me in, I cleaned my arm by sucking it. Afterward, I saw men who hadn't sucked their arms and had terrible holes in them so large I could have pushed my fist through. It was their own fault. They could have sucked.

In my cell was another man who would be my cellmate. He was a young, masculine fellow who didn't talk much, but he was very capable—truly as excellent a person as you could encounter in a day's journey, and this despite the fact that he had just recently completed a two-year sentence in some Ohio penitentiary.

We had barely been in our cell for thirty minutes when a prisoner walked casually down the corridor and peered inside. It was my friend. He had the run of the hall, he told us. He was released from his cell at six in the morning and wasn't locked up again until nine at night. He was connected with the influential group in that hall and had quickly been made a trusty of the type officially called a "hall-man." The person who had given him this position was also an inmate and a trusty, known as the "First Hall-man." There were thirteen hall-men in that hall. Ten of them were each responsible for overseeing a corridor of cells, and above them were the First, Second, and Third Hall-men.

We newcomers had to remain in our cells for the remainder of the day, my friend told me, so the vaccine could take effect. The following morning we would be assigned to hard labor in the prison yard.

"But I'll get you out of that job as soon as I can," he promised. "I'll have one of the hall workers fired and get you hired in his place."

He reached into his shirt, pulled out the handkerchief that held my valuable possessions, handed it to me through the bars, and continued walking down the corridor.

I opened the bundle. Everything was there. Not even a single match was missing. I shared the tobacco for rolling a cigarette with my cellmate. When I began to strike a match to light it, he stopped me. A flimsy, dirty blanket lay on each of our bunks for bedding. He tore off a narrow strip of the thin fabric and rolled it tightly into a long, slender cylinder. He lit this with one of our precious matches. The cylinder of tightly rolled cotton fabric didn't burst into flames. Instead, a glowing ember slowly smoldered at the end. It would burn for hours, and my cellmate called it a "punk." When it burned down too short, all we had to do was make a new punk, touch its end to the old one, blow on them both, and transfer the glowing ember from one to the other. We could have taught Prometheus a thing or two about conserving fire.

At noon, dinner was served. At the bottom of our cell door, there was a small opening similar to the entrance of a chicken coop runway. Through this opening, two chunks of dry bread and two metal cups of "soup" were pushed inside. Each serving of soup contained roughly a quart of hot water with a single drop of grease floating on top. There was also some salt mixed into the water.

We drank the soup, but we left the bread untouched. It wasn't because we lacked appetite, and it wasn't because the bread was inedible. The bread was actually quite decent. But we had our reasons. My cellmate had made a disturbing discovery—our cell was crawling with bedbugs. Massive colonies thrived in every crack and gap between the bricks where the mortar had crumbled away. These creatures were so bold they ventured out in broad daylight, swarming across the walls and ceiling by the hundreds. My cellmate understood these pests well. Like Childe Roland, he fearlessly raised the battle horn to his lips. Never had there been such a fierce fight. The battle raged for hours. It was a complete massacre. When the last survivors retreated to their brick-and-mortar strongholds, our task was only half finished. We chewed chunks of our bread until it became as thick as putty. Whenever a fleeing enemy escaped into a crack between the bricks, we immediately sealed it in with a blob of the chewed bread. We worked tirelessly until the light began to fade and every opening, corner, and crevice was sealed shut. I can't help but shudder when I imagine the horrors of starvation and cannibalism that must have unfolded behind those bread-covered barriers.

We collapsed onto our bunks, exhausted and starving, waiting for our evening meal. It had been a productive day's work, well accomplished. In the coming weeks, we would at least be spared from the swarms of insects and pests. We had skipped our lunch, protecting ourselves at the cost of our empty stomachs, but we felt satisfied. How pointless human efforts can be! We had barely finished our lengthy task when a guard opened our door with his key. The prisoners were being redistributed, and we were moved to a different cell and confined two floors above.

Early the next morning, our cell doors were unlocked, and down in the main hall, several hundred of us prisoners formed a single-file line and marched out into the prison yard to begin our work. The Erie Canal flows directly behind the back yard of the Erie County Penitentiary. Our job was to unload the canal boats, hauling massive stay-bolts on our shoulders, similar to railroad ties, and carrying them into the prison. While I worked, I assessed the situation and examined the possibilities for an escape. There wasn't even the slightest chance. Guards carrying repeating rifles patrolled along the tops of the walls, and I was also informed that machine guns were positioned in the watchtowers.

I wasn't worried. Thirty days wasn't that long. I would stay those thirty days and add to the collection of evidence I planned to use, once I got out, against these vultures of justice. I would show what an American boy could accomplish when his rights and freedoms had been trampled on the way mine had been. I had been denied my right to trial by jury; I had been denied my right to plead guilty or not guilty; I had been denied a trial altogether (since I couldn't consider what I had received at Niagara Falls to be a trial); I had not been allowed to contact a lawyer or anyone else, and therefore had been denied my right to file for a writ of habeas corpus; my face had been shaved, my hair cut short, prison stripes had been placed on my body; I was forced to work hard on a diet of bread and water and to march in the humiliating lock-step with armed guards watching over me—and all for what? What had I done? What crime had I committed against the good citizens of Niagara Falls that all this revenge should be inflicted upon me? I hadn't even violated their "sleeping-out" ordinance. I had slept outside their jurisdiction, in the countryside, that night. I hadn't even begged for a meal, or asked for a "light piece" on their streets. All that I had done was walk along their sidewalk and look at their insignificant waterfall. And what crime was there in that? Technically I was guilty of no wrongdoing. All right, I would show them when I got out.

The following day I spoke with a guard. I wanted to contact a lawyer. The guard laughed at me. The other guards did the same. I truly was cut off from any contact with the outside world. I attempted to write a letter, but I discovered that all correspondence was read and either censored or seized by the prison officials, and that "short-timers" weren't permitted to write letters in any case. Shortly afterward I tried to sneak letters out through men who were being released, but I found out that they were searched and the letters were discovered and destroyed. It didn't matter. All of this would help make my case look worse when I finally got out.

But as the prison days passed (which I will describe in the next chapter), I "learned a few things." I heard stories about the police, police courts, and lawyers that were unbelievable and horrifying.

Men, fellow prisoners, told me about their personal experiences with the police in major cities that were terrible. Even more terrible were the secondhand stories they shared with me about men who had died at the hands of the police and who therefore could not speak for themselves. Years later, in the report of the Lexow Committee, I would read accounts that were true and more terrible than those told to me. But in the meantime, during the first days of my imprisonment, I dismissed what I heard.

As time passed, though, I started to become convinced. I witnessed firsthand, right there in that prison, things that were unbelievable and horrifying. And the more convinced I became, the deeper my respect grew for the detectives of the law and for the entire system of criminal justice.

My anger faded away, and waves of fear flooded through me. I finally saw clearly what I was facing. I became humble and submissive. Every day I decided more firmly to cause no trouble when I was released. All I wanted when I got out was an opportunity to disappear quietly. And that's exactly what I did when they let me go. I kept quiet, moved carefully, and slipped away to Pennsylvania as a wiser and more humble person.

The Pen

For two days I worked in the prison yard. The labor was grueling, and despite the fact that I slacked off whenever I could, I was completely exhausted. This happened because of the food we received. No person could perform hard labor on such meager rations. We were given only bread and water. Once each week we were meant to receive meat, but this meat wasn't always distributed to everyone, and since all the nutrition had already been boiled out of it during soup preparation, it made no difference whether someone got a small portion of it once a week or not.

Furthermore, there was one critical flaw in the bread-and-water diet. While we received plenty of water, we didn't get nearly enough bread. A bread ration was roughly the size of someone's two fists, and each prisoner received three rations daily. There was one positive aspect, I have to admit, about the water—it was hot. In the morning they called it "coffee," at midday it was dignified as "soup," and in the evening it disguised itself as "tea." But it was the same old water every time. The prisoners nicknamed it "water bewitched." In the morning it was black water, the dark color coming from boiling it with burned bread crusts. At noon they served it without the color, with salt and a drop of grease mixed in. In the evening it was served with a purplish-reddish tint that defied any explanation; it was terrible tea, but it made excellent hot water.

We were a starving bunch in the Erie County Pen. Only the "long-timers" understood what it meant to eat enough food. The explanation for this was that they would have eventually died on the meals we "short-timers" were given. I'm certain that the long-timers received more filling food, because there was an entire row of them on the ground floor in our section, and when I became a trusty, I would steal from their food while serving them their meals. A person cannot survive on bread alone, especially when there isn't enough of it.

My friend came through for me. After working in the yard for two days, I was pulled from my cell and promoted to trusty status as a "hall-man." During morning and evening hours, we delivered bread to the prisoners in their individual cells, but the noon meal followed a completely different procedure. The inmates returned from their work assignments marching in a single, extended line. When they reached the entrance to our hall, they abandoned their lock-step formation and dropped their hands from their fellow prisoners' shoulders. Right inside the doorway, stacks of bread trays waited, and this is where the First Hall-man and two regular hall-men positioned themselves. I served as one of those two assistants. Our job involved holding the bread trays while the column of inmates walked past us. The moment my tray became empty, the other hall-man would step in to replace me, carrying a freshly loaded tray. When his tray ran out, I would take over his position with another full tray. This way, the line moved forward at a steady pace, with each man extending his right hand to grab a single bread ration from the outstretched tray.

The First Hall-man had a different job. He carried a club. He positioned himself next to the tray and kept watch. The starving prisoners could never shake the false hope that they might somehow manage to grab two bread rations from the tray. But from what I witnessed, that moment never arrived. The First Hall-man's club would strike out—swift as a tiger's claw—toward any hand that dared to reach too greedily. The First Hall-man was skilled at judging distance, and he had broken so many hands with that club that his aim had become perfect. He never missed his target, and he typically punished the guilty prisoner by confiscating his single ration and sending him back to his cell to survive on nothing but hot water for his meal.

And sometimes, while all these men lay starving in their cells, I witnessed around a hundred extra bread rations stashed away in the cells of the hall-men. It might seem ridiculous that we hoarded this bread. But it was one of our schemes. We were the economic rulers within our hall, pulling off tricks in ways quite similar to the economic rulers of civilization. We controlled the food supply of the population, and, just like our fellow criminals outside, we made the people pay dearly for it. We sold the bread. Once a week, the men who worked in the yard received a five-cent piece of chewing tobacco. This chewing tobacco served as our currency. Two or three bread rations for one plug was how we conducted business, and they made these trades, not because they cared less about tobacco, but because they craved bread more. Oh, I know it was like stealing candy from a baby, but what could we do? We had to survive. And surely there should be some compensation for initiative and enterprise. Besides, we simply copied our superiors outside the walls, who, on a grander scale, and under the respectable mask of merchants, bankers, and captains of industry, did exactly what we were doing. What terrible things would have befallen those poor souls if it hadn't been for us, I cannot imagine. Heaven knows we put bread into circulation in the Erie County Pen. Yes, and we promoted frugality and thrift ... in the poor devils who gave up their tobacco. And then there was our example. In the heart of every convict there we planted the desire to become just like us and run a scheme. Saviours of society—I guess yes.

Here was a starving man who had run out of tobacco. Perhaps he had been reckless and consumed it all himself. That was fine; he owned a pair of suspenders. I traded six bread rations for them—or twelve rations if the suspenders were of excellent quality. I never used suspenders myself, but that was irrelevant. Around the corner lived a long-term prisoner, serving ten years for manslaughter. He used suspenders and needed a new pair. I could exchange them with him for some of his meat. Meat was exactly what I needed. Or maybe he possessed a worn, paperback novel. That would be like finding treasure. I could read it and then trade it to the bakers for cake, or to the cooks for meat and vegetables, or to the firemen for good coffee, or to someone else for the newspaper that sometimes made its way inside, God only knows how. The cooks, bakers, and firemen were inmates just like me, and they lived in our hall in the first row of cells above us.

In short, a complete bartering system operated throughout the Erie County Penitentiary. Real money was even circulating within the prison. This money was occasionally brought in by inmates serving brief sentences, more often originated from the barbershop scam where new prisoners were cheated, but primarily came from the cells of long-term inmates—though I have no idea how they obtained it.

What about his superior position? The First Hall-man was known to be quite wealthy. Beyond his various schemes, he took advantage of us as well. We cultivated the general misery, and the First Hall-man served as the Chief Overseer of all of us. We maintained our individual schemes with his approval, and we were required to pay for that approval. As I mentioned, he was known to be wealthy; however, we never witnessed his money, and he lived alone in a cell in isolated splendor.

But that money was earned in the prison, and I had direct proof of this because I shared a cell for quite some time with the Third Hall-man. He possessed more than sixteen dollars. Every night after nine o'clock, when we were locked in our cells, he would count his money. He also told me each night what he would do to me if I revealed his secret to the other hall-men. You see, he was terrified of being robbed, and danger came at him from three different directions. First, there were the guards. A couple of them might attack him, beat him severely for supposed disobedience, and throw him into solitary confinement (the dungeon); and during that chaos, his sixteen dollars would disappear. Then there was the First Hall-man, who could have taken everything from him by threatening to fire him and send him back to hard labor in the prison yard. And finally, there were the ten of us who were regular hall-men. If we discovered his wealth, there was a strong chance that on some quiet day, all of us would corner him and take him down. Oh, we were predators, believe me—just like the men who conduct business on Wall Street.

He had every reason to fear us, just as I had every reason to fear him. He was an enormous, uneducated savage, a former oyster pirate from Chesapeake Bay, an ex-convict who had served five years in Sing Sing, and an all-around mindlessly vicious animal. He would catch sparrows that flew into our corridor through the open bars. Whenever he caught one, he would rush back to his cell with it, where I witnessed him crushing bones and spitting out feathers as he devoured it alive. No, I never betrayed him to the other inmates in our block. This marks the first time I've ever spoken of his sixteen dollars.

But I took advantage of him anyway. He was in love with a female prisoner who was locked up in the "women's section." He couldn't read or write, so I would read her letters to him and write his responses. And I charged him for it, too. But they were excellent letters. I put my heart into them, gave them my best effort, and what's more, I won her over for him; though I have a strong suspicion that she fell in love, not with him, but with the anonymous writer. I say again, those letters were outstanding.

Another one of our schemes was "passing the punk." We were the heavenly messengers, the fire-carriers, in that iron world of locks and bars. When the men returned from work at night and were locked in their cells, they wanted to smoke. That's when we brought back the divine spark, running through the galleries, from cell to cell, with our smoldering punks. Those who were smart, or who we did business with, had their punks ready to light. Not everyone received divine sparks, though. The guy who refused to pay up went without sparks and smoke to bed. But what did we care? We had the ultimate advantage over him, and if he got mouthy, two or three of us would jump on him and give him what he deserved.

You see, this was how the hall-men operated. There were thirteen of us. We had roughly five hundred prisoners in our hall. We were expected to do the work and maintain order. The second responsibility belonged to the guards, but they handed it over to us. It was our job to keep things under control; if we failed, we'd be sent back to hard labor, most likely with some time in the dungeon added on. But as long as we maintained order, we could continue running our own specific schemes.

Please bear with me for a moment and consider the situation we faced. There were thirteen of us overseeing more than five hundred other inmates. That prison was a living nightmare, and it fell to us thirteen to maintain control. Given the nature of these men, ruling through kindness was simply impossible. We had to rule through fear. Naturally, the guards stood behind us as our backup. In desperate situations, we would call on them for assistance; however, bothering them too frequently would only irritate them, and we could count on them replacing us with more capable trustees if we did. We rarely called upon them, except in a discreet manner when we needed a cell opened to reach a defiant prisoner inside. In those instances, the guard would simply unlock the door and walk away to avoid witnessing what occurred when half a dozen hall-men entered and administered some physical persuasion.

Regarding the specifics of this physical abuse, I won't say anything more. After all, physical abuse was just one of the very minor unpublishable horrors of the Erie County Pen. I say "unpublishable," and in fairness I must also say "unimaginable."

These things were unimaginable to me until I witnessed them, and I was no inexperienced person when it came to the ways of the world and the terrible depths of human degradation. It would take a deep measuring line to reach the bottom in the Erie County Pen, and I only touch lightly and casually on the surface of things as I observed them there.

At times, like in the morning when the prisoners came down to wash, the thirteen of us would be practically alone surrounded by them, and every single one of them had it out for us. Thirteen against five hundred, and we maintained control through fear. We couldn't allow the smallest violation of rules, the slightest disrespect. If we did, we were finished. Our own rule was to strike a man the moment he opened his mouth—strike him hard, strike him with whatever was available. A broom handle, end-first, to the face, had a very sobering effect. But that wasn't everything. Such a man had to be made an example of; so the next rule was to charge right in and pursue him. Of course, one could be certain that every hall-man in sight would come running to join in the punishment; for this was also a rule. Whenever any hall-man was in conflict with a prisoner, the responsibility of any other hall-man who happened to be nearby was to lend a hand. Never mind the details of the situation—charge in and strike, and strike with anything; in short, knock the man down.

I remember a handsome young mixed-race man of about twenty who got the crazy idea in his head that he should stand up for his rights. And he was right to do so; but that didn't help him at all. He lived on the highest floor. Eight guards knocked that notion out of him in just about a minute and a half—that's how long it took to drag him along his corridor to the end and down five flights of steel stairs. He traveled the entire distance on every part of his body except his feet, and the eight guards kept busy the whole time. The young man hit the pavement where I was standing watching it all happen. He got back on his feet and stood upright for a moment. In that moment he threw his arms wide and let out a terrible scream of terror and pain and heartbreak. At the same instant, like in a magic trick, the torn pieces of his thick prison clothes fell away from him, leaving him completely naked and bleeding from every part of his body. Then he collapsed in a heap, unconscious. He had learned his lesson, and every prisoner within those walls who heard him scream had learned a lesson too. I had learned mine as well. It's not a pleasant thing to watch a man's spirit get broken in a minute and a half.

The following will show how we built up business in the racket of sharing the punk. A line of new inmates gets placed in your cells. You walk past the bars carrying your punk. "Hey, buddy, give us a light," someone calls out to you. This serves as an advertisement that this particular guy has tobacco on him. You pass the punk through and continue on your way. A short while later you return and lean casually against the bars. "Say, buddy, can you spare us a little tobacco?" is what you ask. If he doesn't understand the game, chances are he seriously insists that he doesn't have any more tobacco. That's fine. You sympathize with him and move on. But you know his punk will only last him for the remainder of that day. The next day you walk by, and he calls out again, "Hey, buddy, give us a light." And you respond, "You don't have any tobacco and you don't need a light." And you don't give him one, either. Thirty minutes later, or an hour or two or three hours afterward, you'll be walking past and the man will call out to you in gentle tones, "Come here, buddy." And you approach. You stick your hand between the bars and have it filled with valuable tobacco. Then you give him a light.

Sometimes, though, a new prisoner shows up who isn't going to be targeted for any schemes. Word gets passed around mysteriously that this guy needs to be treated with respect. I never could figure out where this message came from originally. What's obvious is that the man has connections. Maybe it's with one of the senior inmates who run things; maybe it's with one of the guards in another section of the prison; maybe decent treatment has been bought and paid for through corrupt officials higher up the chain; but whatever the case, we understand that we need to treat him right if we want to stay out of trouble.

We hall-men served as intermediaries and go-betweens. We set up trades between prisoners locked up in different sections of the prison, and we carried out the exchanges. We also collected our fees on both ends of the deal. Sometimes the items being traded had to pass through the hands of half a dozen middlemen, each one taking his cut or getting paid for his services in one way or another.

Sometimes people owed favors for services, and sometimes they had others who owed them. So when I arrived at the prison, I was indebted to the convict who had smuggled my belongings inside for me. About a week later, one of the firemen slipped a letter into my hand. A barber had given it to him. The barber had gotten it from the convict who had brought in my things. Because I owed him a favor, I was supposed to pass the letter along. But he hadn't written the letter himself. The person who originally sent it was a long-term prisoner in his section. The letter was meant for a woman prisoner in the women's section. But I didn't know whether it was actually intended for her, or if she was just another link in the chain of messengers. All I knew was what she looked like, and that my job was to get the letter to her.

Two days went by, and I kept the letter with me the entire time. Then the chance I'd been waiting for finally arrived. The women prisoners were responsible for mending all the clothing worn by the inmates. Several men from our hall had to go to the women's section to collect large bundles of repaired clothes. I arranged with the First Hall-man to be included in this group. One door after another was unlocked as we made our way through the prison corridors to reach the women's quarters. We walked into a spacious room where the women sat busy with their sewing work. I scanned the room carefully, searching for the woman who had been described to me. I spotted her and maneuvered myself close to where she was working. Two sharp-eyed female guards were keeping watch over everything. I concealed the letter in my palm and caught the woman's eye to signal my purpose. She understood that I had something for her—she must have been anticipating this delivery and had been trying to figure out, from the moment we walked in, which one of us was carrying her message. However, one of the guards was standing less than two feet away from her. The hall-men were already gathering up the bundles they needed to take back with them. The crucial moment was slipping away. I stalled with my bundle, pretending that the ties weren't secure enough. Would that guard ever look in another direction? Was I going to fail in this mission? Right then, another woman started fooling around with one of the hall-men—she stuck her foot out to trip him, or gave him a pinch, or pulled some other prank. The guard turned her attention that way and scolded the woman harshly. I still don't know if this distraction was deliberately planned to draw the guard's focus away, but I certainly knew this was my chance. My target woman let her hand fall from her lap down to her side. I bent down to grab my bundle. From my crouched position, I slipped the letter into her waiting hand and took another letter from her in return. The next instant, the bundle was hoisted onto my shoulder, the guard's attention had shifted back to me since I was the last hall-man still there, and I was hurrying to catch up with my fellow inmates. The letter I had received from the woman went to the fireman, and from there it traveled through the hands of the barber, then to the convict who had smuggled in my belongings, and finally reached the long-timer at the far end of the chain.

Often we carried letters through a communication network so complicated that we didn't know who was sending them or who would receive them. We were simply links in the chain. At some point, somehow, a prisoner would slip a letter into my hand with instructions to pass it along to the next person in line. All these actions were favors that would be returned later, when I would be working directly with someone important in sending letters, and from whom I would receive my payment. The entire prison was covered by a web of communication lines. And we who controlled the communication system naturally charged our customers heavy fees, since we were modeled after capitalist society. It was service for profit with a vengeance, though we sometimes weren't above providing service out of kindness.

During my entire time in the penitentiary, I was building a strong relationship with my cellmate. He had helped me considerably, and in exchange he expected me to do the same for him. When we were released, we planned to travel together and, naturally, carry out criminal activities as partners. My cellmate was a criminal—not a mastermind by any means, just a small-time offender who would steal and rob, break into homes, and if trapped, wouldn't hesitate to kill. We spent many peaceful hours sitting and talking together. He had several criminal schemes planned for the near future, where my role was already determined, and I participated in working out the specifics. I had spent time around criminals and observed them closely, so my cellmate never suspected that I was deceiving him, leading him on for thirty days straight. He believed I was genuine, appreciated me because I wasn't foolish, and I think he also liked me as a person. Naturally, I had absolutely no intention of joining him in a life of miserable, small-time crime; but I would have been a fool to waste all the benefits his friendship provided. When someone finds himself on the burning lava of hell, he cannot be selective about his route, and that was my situation in the Erie County Penitentiary. I had to remain in good standing with the gang, or face hard labor on bread and water; and to stay in good standing with the gang I had to maintain my relationship with my cellmate.

Life wasn't boring in the prison. Something happened every day: inmates were having seizures, losing their minds, getting into fights, or the trustees were getting drunk. Rover Jack, one of the regular trustees, was our main troublemaker. He was a genuine professional criminal, a career convict through and through, and because of this the trustees in charge gave him plenty of leeway. Pittsburgh Joe, who served as Second Trustee, would join Rover Jack on his drinking binges; and the two of them used to say that the Erie County Penitentiary was the only place where a man could get completely drunk without being arrested. I never found out for certain, but I heard that potassium bromide, obtained through sneaky means from the medical dispensary, was the substance they used. But I can confirm that whatever their drug of choice was, they definitely got thoroughly intoxicated from time to time.

Our hall was a common cesspool, filled with society's refuse and filth, the lowest dregs of humanity—those born inadequate, the degenerate, the broken, the insane, those with damaged minds, epileptics, grotesque beings, the weak, in essence, a living nightmare of human existence. Consequently, seizures were rampant among us. These seizures appeared to spread from person to person. When one man started having a seizure, others would follow suit. I witnessed seven men simultaneously suffering from seizures, their screams making the air terrible to hear, while just as many other mentally ill patients would be raging and babbling frantically throughout the space. The only treatment ever provided for those having seizures was to douse them with cold water. It was pointless to call for the medical student or physician. They refused to be disturbed by such minor and routine incidents.

There was a young Dutch boy, around eighteen years old, who suffered from seizures more often than anyone else. He typically had one every day. Because of this, we housed him on the ground floor further along the corridor of cells where we were kept. After he experienced several seizures in the prison yard, the guards decided they didn't want to deal with him anymore, so he stayed locked in his cell all day with a Cockney cellmate for company. The Cockney wasn't much help, though. Every time the Dutch boy had a seizure, the Cockney would freeze up in complete fear.

The Dutch boy couldn't speak any English at all. He was a farm worker's son, serving a ninety-day sentence as punishment for getting into a fight with someone. His seizures always began with howling. He howled like a wild wolf. He also had his seizures while standing upright, which created serious problems for him, because his episodes always ended with him falling headfirst to the ground. Whenever I heard that long, wolf-like howl beginning, I would grab a broom and rush to his cell. The trusties weren't given keys to the cells, so I couldn't get inside to help him. He would stand in the center of his cramped cell, shaking uncontrollably, his eyes rolled back so far that only the white parts showed, howling like a damned spirit. No matter how hard I tried, I could never convince the Cockney to help him. While the Dutch boy stood there howling, the Cockney huddled and shook in the top bunk, his frightened eyes locked on that terrifying figure with the rolled-back eyes who just kept howling and howling. It was tough on the Cockney too, the poor bastard. His own mental state wasn't very stable to begin with, and it's amazing that he didn't lose his mind completely.

All I could do was my best with the broom. I would push it through the bars, aim it at Dutchy's chest, and wait. As the seizure approached, he would start swaying back and forth. I followed this swaying motion with the broom, since there was no way to predict when he would take that terrible forward fall. But when he did, I was ready with the broom, catching him and helping him down gently. No matter how hard I tried, he never landed softly, and his face usually got bruised against the stone floor. Once he was down and writhing in convulsions, I'd splash a bucket of water over him.

I don't know if cold water was the right treatment or not, but that was the standard practice at the Erie County Pen. Nothing more was ever done for him. He would lie there, soaking wet, for about an hour, and then crawl into his bunk. I knew better than to run to a guard for help. What did a man having a seizure matter, anyway?

In the cell next door lived an unusual character—a man who was serving sixty days for eating scraps from Barnum's garbage barrel, or at least that's how he described it. He was a severely confused person, and initially, very calm and gentle. The details of his situation were exactly as he had explained them. He had wandered onto the circus grounds, and being hungry, had found his way to the barrel that held the leftover food from the circus workers' meals. "And it was good bread," he frequently told me; "and the meat was excellent." A police officer had spotted him and arrested him, and there he was.

Once I walked past his cell carrying a piece of stiff, thin wire in my hand. He begged me for it so desperately that I slipped it through the bars to him. Immediately, using nothing but his fingers as tools, he snapped it into short pieces and twisted them into half a dozen quite impressive safety pins. He sharpened the points against the stone floor. From that point on, I ran a profitable safety pin business. I provided the raw materials and sold the finished products, while he handled the manufacturing. As payment, I gave him extra bread rations, and occasionally a piece of meat or a soup bone with some marrow still inside.

But his time in prison affected him deeply, and he became more violent with each passing day. The guards enjoyed tormenting him. They filled his fragile mind with tales of a vast inheritance that belonged to him. They told him he had been arrested and thrown in jail so they could steal this fortune from him. Naturally, as he well understood, there was no crime in eating from a barrel. This meant his imprisonment was unjust. It was all a scheme to steal his wealth.

The first time I became aware of it, I heard the attendants laughing about how they had been deceiving him. Then he held a serious meeting with me, during which he told me about his millions and the conspiracy to steal them from him, and he appointed me as his detective. I did everything I could to let him down easy, speaking in vague terms about a misunderstanding, and explaining that it was another man with a similar name who was the true heir. I left him feeling much calmer; but I couldn't keep the attendants away from him, and they kept deceiving him even more than before. Eventually, after an extremely violent confrontation, he knocked me down, fired me from my private detective position, and went on strike. My business in safety pins came to an end. He refused to make any more safety pins, and he pelted me with raw materials through the bars of his cell whenever I walked past.

I could never reconcile with him. The other inmates told him that I was a detective working for the conspirators. Meanwhile, the inmates tormented him relentlessly with their harassment. His imaginary grievances consumed his thoughts, and eventually he became a dangerous and murderous madman. The guards refused to believe his story about stolen millions, and he accused them of being part of the conspiracy. One day he threw a cup of hot tea at one of them, and then his situation was examined. The warden spoke with him briefly through the bars of his cell. Then he was taken away for evaluation by the doctors. He never returned, and I often wonder whether he is dead, or if he still rambles about his millions in some mental institution.

At last came the day of days, my release. It was also the day of release for the Third Hall-man, and the short-timer girl I had secured for him was waiting for him outside the wall. They departed blissfully together. My friend and I left together, and together we walked down into Buffalo. Weren't we supposed to stay together always? We panhandled together on the main street that day for coins, and whatever we collected was spent on small glasses of beer—I'm not sure how they're spelled, but they're pronounced the way I've written them, and they cost three cents each. I was looking for my opportunity the entire time to escape. From some vagrant on the street I managed to find out what time a particular freight train departed. I planned my timing accordingly. When the moment arrived, my friend and I were in a bar. Two foaming small beers sat before us. I would have liked to say goodbye. He had been kind to me. But I didn't dare. I slipped out through the back of the bar and jumped the fence. It was a quick escape, and a few minutes later I was aboard a freight train and heading south on the Western New York and Pennsylvania Railroad.

Hoboes That Pass in the Night

During my travels as a hobo, I met hundreds of other drifters who either called out to me or whom I greeted, and with whom I waited by water tanks, cleaned up, prepared stew, begged from freight trains or private homes, and rode the rails illegally, and who then moved on and were never encountered again. On the other hand, there were hoboes who came and went with remarkable regularity, and still others who passed by like phantoms, nearby yet invisible, never to be spotted.

It was one of these wanderers that I pursued all the way across Canada, covering over three thousand miles by railroad, yet I never once caught sight of him. His "monica" was Skysail Jack. I first encountered it in Montreal. Carved with a jack-knife was the skysail-yard of a ship. The carving was perfectly executed. Below it was "Skysail Jack." Above was "B.W. 9-15-94." This marking told me that he had traveled through Montreal heading west on October 15, 1894. He had a one-day head start on me. "Sailor Jack" was my monica at that time, and I immediately carved it next to his, along with the date and the information that I was also heading west.

I ran into bad luck covering the next hundred miles, and eight days later I found Skysail Jack's trail three hundred miles west of Ottawa. There it was, carved into a water tank, and from the date I could see that he had also faced delays. He was only two days ahead of me. I was a "comet" and "tramp-royal," and so was Skysail Jack; my pride and reputation demanded that I catch up with him. I rode the rails day and night, and I passed him; then he turned around and passed me. Sometimes he was a day or so ahead, and sometimes I was. From hoboes heading east, I occasionally got news of him when he happened to be ahead; and from them I discovered that he had become curious about Sailor Jack and was asking questions about me.

We would have made quite a pair, I'm certain, if we had ever managed to meet up; but meeting up was impossible for us. I stayed ahead of him all the way across Manitoba, but he took the lead crossing Alberta, and early one bitterly cold gray morning, at the end of a rail division just east of Kicking Horse Pass, I discovered that he had been spotted the previous night somewhere between Kicking Horse Pass and Rogers' Pass. The way this information reached me was rather strange. I had been traveling all night in a "side-door Pullman" (freight car), and nearly frozen to death, I had crawled out at the division to ask for food. A freezing mist was drifting by, and I approached some railroad workers I found in the engine house. They helped me out with the leftovers from their lunch boxes, and on top of that I managed to get nearly a quart of wonderful "Java" (coffee) from them. I warmed up the coffee, and as I sat down to eat, a freight train arrived from the west. I watched a side door open and a young drifter climb out. Through the drifting fog he hobbled over to me. He was rigid with cold, his lips turned blue. I shared my Java and food with him, found out about Skysail Jack, and then learned about him. As it turned out, he was from my own hometown, Oakland, California, and he belonged to the famous Boo Gang— a gang I had joined up with on occasional occasions. We talked rapidly and wolfed down the food during the half-hour that followed. Then my freight train departed, and I was aboard it, heading west on the trail of Skysail Jack.

I got held up in the mountain passes, went without eating for two days, and had to walk eleven miles on the third day before I found any food. Despite all that, I managed to overtake Skysail Jack somewhere along the Fraser River in British Columbia. I was catching rides on freight trains at the time, trying to make good time, but he must have been doing the same thing with better luck or more skill than me, because he reached Mission before I did.

Now Mission was a junction, forty miles east of Vancouver. From the junction one could travel south through Washington and Oregon via the Northern Pacific. I wondered which direction Skysail Jack would take, since I believed I was ahead of him. As for me, I was still heading west to Vancouver. I went to the water tank to leave that information, and there, freshly carved with that day's date on it, was Skysail Jack's signature. I rushed on into Vancouver. But he was gone. He had boarded a ship immediately and was still flying west on his world adventure. Truly, Skysail Jack, you were a genuine tramp, and your companion was the "wind that tramps the world." I tip my hat to you. You were the real deal, all right. A week later I also got my ship, and aboard the steamship Umatilla, in the crew quarters, I was working my way down the coast to San Francisco. Skysail Jack and Sailor Jack—wow! if we had ever met up.

Water tanks serve as directories for hobos. Tramps don't carve their nicknames, dates, and routes just for fun or out of boredom. Time and again, I've encountered drifters asking earnestly whether I'd seen a particular "guy" or his nickname anywhere. More than once, I've been able to provide a recently carved nickname, the specific water tank where I saw it, and the direction the person was heading. Right away, the hobo I shared this information with would take off to find his friend. I've come across drifters who, while trying to catch up with a buddy, had chased him all the way across the country and back, and were still searching.

"Monicas" are the nicknames that hoboes take on or have given to them by their fellow travelers. Leary Joe, for example, was a fearful person, and received this name from his companions. No hobo with any pride would choose a name like Stew Bum for himself. Very few wanderers want to recall their past lives when they worked regular jobs, so nicknames based on former occupations are uncommon, though I do remember meeting these individuals: Moulder Blackey, Painter Red, Chi Plumber, Boiler-Maker, Sailor Boy, and Printer Bo. "Chi" (pronounced shy), incidentally, is slang for "Chicago."

A popular method hoboes use is to create their nicknames based on the places they come from, such as: New York Tommy, Pacific Slim, Buffalo Smithy, Canton Tim, Pittsburgh Jack, Syracuse Shine, Troy Mickey, K.L. Bill, and Connecticut Jimmy. There was also "Slim Jim from Vinegar Hill, who never worked and never will." A "shine" always refers to a Black person, called this way, perhaps, because of the highlights on their face. Texas Shine or Toledo Shine indicate both race and place of origin.

Among those who adopted names based on their ethnicity, I remember these individuals: Frisco Sheeny, New York Irish, Michigan French, English Jack, Cockney Kid, and Milwaukee Dutch. Others appeared to derive their nicknames partly from the physical characteristics they were born with, including: Chi Whitey, New Jersey Red, Boston Blackey, Seattle Browney, and Yellow Dick and Yellow Belly—the latter being a Creole from Mississippi who, I believe, had his nickname forced upon him.

Texas Royal, Happy Joe, Bust Connors, Burley Bo, Tornado Blackey, and Touch McCall showed more creativity when they gave themselves new names. Others, with less imagination, adopted names based on their physical characteristics, such as: Vancouver Slim, Detroit Shorty, Ohio Fatty, Long Jack, Big Jim, Little Joe, New York Blink, Chi Nosey, and Broken-backed Ben.

The Road-kids arrive on their own, each carrying a vast array of nicknames. For instance, I've come across the following individuals during my travels: Buck Kid, Blind Kid, Midget Kid, Holy Kid, Bat Kid, Swift Kid, Cookey Kid, Monkey Kid, Iowa Kid, Corduroy Kid, Orator Kid (who had quite a story about how he got his name), and Lippy Kid (who was definitely mouthy, you could count on that).

On the water tank at San Marcial, New Mexico, twelve years ago, there was the following hobo menu:

1. The main street is fair for opportunities.
2. The police officers are not hostile.
3. The railroad roundhouse is good for sleeping.
4. Northbound trains are not good for riding.
5. Private homes are not good for help.
6. Restaurants are good only for those seeking work as cooks.
7. The Railroad House is good only for nighttime work.

The first symbol indicates that asking for money on the main street is acceptable; the second shows that police won't hassle drifters; the third reveals that sleeping in the roundhouse is possible. The fourth symbol, though, remains unclear. The northbound trains might be difficult to hop, or they could be poor prospects for panhandling. The fifth marking warns that residential areas aren't welcoming to beggars, while the sixth indicates that only wanderers with cooking experience can obtain food from restaurants. The seventh symbol puzzles me. I can't determine whether the Railroad House welcomes any drifter seeking handouts at night, or if it's only favorable to those with cooking skills who beg after dark, or whether any wanderer, regardless of culinary background, can offer assistance during nighttime hours, helping the Railroad House kitchen staff with menial tasks in exchange for a meal.

But to return to the drifters who pass through in the night. I remember one I encountered in California. He was Swedish, but he had lived in the United States for so long that you couldn't tell where he was from. He had to reveal it himself. In fact, he had arrived in the United States as just a baby. I first came across him in the mountain town of Truckee. "Which way, friend?" was how we greeted each other, and "Heading east" was the response we both gave. Quite a group of wanderers attempted to catch a ride on the transcontinental train that night, and I lost track of the Swede in all the commotion. I also missed the train.

I arrived in Reno, Nevada, in a freight car that was immediately moved to a side track. It was a Sunday morning, and after I begged for breakfast, I walked over to the Paiute camp to watch the Native Americans gambling. And there stood the Swede, deeply fascinated. Naturally we came together. He was the only person I knew in that area, and I was his only acquaintance. We rushed toward each other like a pair of lonely hermits, and together we spent the day, begged for our dinner, and late in the afternoon attempted to catch the same freight train. But he was left behind, and I rode it out alone, only to be left behind myself in the desert twenty miles further on.

Of all the desolate places where someone could be abandoned, this one was absolutely the worst. It was called a flag-station, and it consisted of nothing more than a shack carelessly dropped into the sand and sagebrush. A cold wind was blowing, darkness was approaching, and the lone telegraph operator who lived in the shack was terrified of me. I knew I wouldn't be able to get either food or a place to sleep from him. It was precisely because of his obvious fear of me that I didn't believe him when he told me that eastbound trains never stopped there. After all, hadn't I just been thrown off an eastbound train at that exact spot less than five minutes earlier? He assured me that it had stopped under special orders, and that a year might pass before another would be stopped under orders. He suggested that it was only twelve or fifteen miles to Wadsworth and that I should walk there. I chose to wait, however, and I had the satisfaction of watching two westbound freight trains pass by without stopping, along with one eastbound freight. I wondered if the Swede was on that last one. It was up to me to walk the railroad ties to Wadsworth, and walk them I did, much to the telegraph operator's relief, since I chose not to burn down his shack and kill him. Telegraph operators have much to be grateful for. After walking about six miles, I had to get off the tracks and let the eastbound passenger train go by. It was moving fast, but I caught a glimpse of a shadowy figure on the first "blind" car that looked like the Swede.

That was the last time I saw him for many long days. I traveled through the high country across those hundreds of miles of Nevada desert, taking the overland routes at night for speed, and during the day riding in freight cars to get some sleep. It was early in the year, and the weather was cold in those highland areas. Snow covered patches of flat ground here and there, all the mountains were wrapped in white, and at night the most bitter wind you could imagine swept down from them. This was not a place where anyone would want to stay long. And remember, dear reader, the hobo travels through such territory without shelter, without money, begging for food and sleeping at night without blankets. This final point is something that can only be truly understood through personal experience.

In the early evening I arrived at the depot in Ogden. The Union Pacific overland train was heading east, and I was determined to make my connection. Out in the maze of railroad tracks in front of the locomotive, I came across a figure shuffling through the darkness. It was the Swede. We shook hands like long-lost brothers and noticed that we were both wearing gloves. "Where did you get them?" I asked. "From an engine cab," he replied, "and where did you get yours?" "They belonged to a fireman," I said, "he wasn't paying attention."

We caught the freight train as it pulled away from the station, and we found it extremely cold. The route climbed through a narrow canyon between snow-covered mountains, and we trembled from the cold while sharing stories about how we had traveled the distance between Reno and Ogden. I had only slept for about an hour the night before, and riding on the freight train wasn't comfortable enough for me to take a nap. When the train stopped, I walked forward to the locomotive. We had two engines pulling the train to get us over the mountain pass.

The engineer's position on the lead locomotive would be too cold since it had to "punch through the wind," so I chose the engineer's spot on the second locomotive, which was protected by the first one. I climbed onto the cowcatcher and discovered someone was already occupying the pilot area. In the darkness, I felt around and found the shape of a young boy who was fast asleep. By squeezing together, there was enough space for both of us on the pilot, so I nudged the boy over and climbed up next to him. It turned out to be a "good" night; the "shacks" (brakemen) left us alone, and before long we had fallen asleep. Occasionally, burning cinders or rough jolts would wake me up, and I would press closer to the boy and drift back to sleep to the sound of the engines coughing and the wheels screeching.

The overland train reached Evanston, Wyoming, and couldn't go any further. A wreck up ahead had blocked the railway line. They had brought in the body of the dead engineer, and his corpse served as evidence of how dangerous this route was. A tramp had also been killed, but they hadn't retrieved his body. I spoke with the boy. He was thirteen years old. He had run away from his family somewhere in Oregon and was traveling east to reach his grandmother. He told me a story about the cruel treatment he had endured in the home he'd left behind, and it sounded genuine; furthermore, he had no reason to lie to me, just another anonymous hobo on the rails.

And that boy was really moving fast. He couldn't travel across the ground quickly enough. When the division supervisors decided to send the overland train back the way it had traveled, then up on a connecting route to the Oregon Short Line, and back along that railroad to connect with the Union Pacific on the other side of the wreck, that boy climbed onto the front of the locomotive and said he was going to stay with it. This was too much for the Swede and me. It meant traveling the rest of that freezing night just to gain no more than about twelve miles or so. We said we'd wait until the wreck was cleared away, and in the meantime get some good sleep.

Finding a place to sleep in an unfamiliar town at midnight during cold weather when you're completely broke is no easy task. The Swede was completely penniless. All the money I had was two dimes and a nickel. Some local guys told us that beer cost five cents and the bars stayed open all night. That was our solution. Two beers would run us ten cents, and there would be a heater and chairs where we could sleep until morning. We walked quickly toward the glowing lights of a bar, snow crunching beneath our feet while a sharp, cold wind cut right through us.

Unfortunately, I had misunderstood the local boys. Beer cost five cents in only one saloon in the entire town, and we didn't find that particular saloon. However, the one we entered was perfectly fine. A wonderful stove was blazing white-hot; there were comfortable, cane-bottomed armchairs, and a rather unpleasant-looking bartender who stared at us suspiciously as we walked in. A person cannot spend days and nights continuously in the same clothes, hopping trains, battling soot and ash, and sleeping wherever possible, while still maintaining a respectable appearance. Our appearances were definitely working against us; but what did we care? I had the money in my pocket.

"Two beers," I said casually to the bartender, and while he poured them, the Swede and I leaned against the bar and secretly longed for the armchairs by the stove.

The bartender placed the two foaming glasses in front of us, and I proudly put down the ten cents. Now I was completely committed. As soon as I realized my mistake about the price, I would have found another ten cents. It didn't matter if it left me with only a nickel to my name, a stranger in an unfamiliar place. I would have paid it without question. But that bartender never gave me the opportunity. The moment his eyes caught sight of the dime

I had placed on the bar, he grabbed the two glasses, one in each hand, and poured the beer into the sink behind the counter. At the same time, glaring at us with hostility, he said:—

"You have scabs on your nose. You have scabs on your nose. You have scabs on your nose. Look!"

I hadn't either, and the Swede hadn't either. Our noses were perfectly fine. We couldn't grasp the direct meaning of what he was saying, but the underlying message was crystal clear: he didn't approve of our appearance, and apparently beer cost ten cents per glass.

I reached into my pocket and placed another dime on the bar, commenting casually, "Oh, I thought this was a five-cent place."

"Your money's no good here," he replied, pushing the two dimes across the bar toward me.

Sadly I put them back in my pocket, sadly we longed for the wonderful stove and the armchairs, and sadly we walked out the door into the freezing night.

But as we walked out the door, the bartender, still glaring, shouted after us, "You've got scabs on your nose, you know!"

I have seen much of the world since then, traveled among unfamiliar lands and peoples, read many books, and attended countless lectures; but to this day, despite thinking long and hard about it, I have been unable to figure out the meaning behind the mysterious words of that bartender in Evanston, Wyoming. Our noses were perfectly fine.

We spent that night sleeping above the boilers in an electric power plant. I can't recall how we found that sleeping spot. We must have simply made our way there by instinct, the way horses naturally find water or homing pigeons return to their roost. But it was a night I'd rather forget. A dozen drifters had already claimed the space on top of the boilers before we arrived, and the area was too cramped and overheated for all of us. To make matters worse, the plant engineer wouldn't allow us to loiter on the ground level below. He gave us an ultimatum: either sleep on the boilers or brave the snow outside.

"You said you wanted to sleep, so damn it, sleep," he told me when I came down to the engine room, frantic and exhausted from the heat.

"Water," I gasped, wiping the sweat from my eyes, "water."

He gestured toward the door and promised me that somewhere down there in the darkness I would find the river. I headed toward the river, became lost in the dark, tumbled into two or three snowdrifts, abandoned the effort, and came back half-frozen to the top of the boilers. After I had warmed up, I felt thirstier than before. All around me the hoboes were moaning, groaning, sobbing, sighing, gasping, panting, rolling and tossing and struggling heavily in their misery. We resembled countless lost souls burning on a hot plate in hell, and the engineer, like Satan himself, offered us only the choice of freezing in the bitter cold outside. The Swede sat up and cursed with intense feeling the restless urge in people that drives them to wander and endure such terrible hardships.

"When I get back to Chicago," he declared emphatically, "I'm going to find a job and stick with it until the end of time. Then I'll go wandering again."

And, such is the irony of fate, the next day, when the wreck ahead was cleared, the Swede and I pulled out of Evanston in the ice-boxes of an "orange special," a fast freight train loaded with fruit from sunny California. Of course, the ice-boxes were empty because of the cold weather, but that didn't make them any warmer for us. We entered them through hatchways in the top of the car; the boxes were made of galvanized iron, and in that bitter weather were not pleasant to touch. We lay there, shivering and shaking, and with chattering teeth held a discussion where we decided that we'd stay by the ice-boxes day and night until we got out of the unwelcoming plateau region and down into the

Mississippi Valley.

But we had to eat, and we decided that at the next stop we would get off to find food and then hurry back to our refrigerator cars. We reached the town of Green River late in the afternoon, but it was still too early for supper. The time before meals is the worst time for begging at back doors, but we gathered our courage, jumped off the side ladders as the freight train pulled into the rail yards, and ran toward the houses. We quickly got separated, but we had agreed to meet back at the refrigerator cars. I had bad luck at first, but eventually, with a couple of handouts stuffed into my shirt, I ran back toward the train. It was already pulling out and picking up speed. The specific refrigerator car where we were supposed to meet had already passed by, so I grabbed onto the side ladders of a car that was half a dozen cars further down the train, climbed up on top quickly, and dropped down into a refrigerator car.

But a railroad worker had spotted me from the caboose, and at the next stop a few miles down the line, Rock Springs, the worker poked his head into my boxcar and shouted: "Get off the train, you worthless bum! Get off now!" He also seized me by the ankles and pulled me out. I certainly got off the train, and the orange freight train and the Swedish man continued on their journey without me.

Snow was starting to fall. A cold night was approaching. Once darkness fell, I searched through the railroad yards until I discovered an empty refrigerator car. I climbed inside—not into the ice compartments, but into the main car itself. I pulled the heavy doors closed, and their edges, lined with rubber strips, made the car completely airtight. The walls were thick. There was no way for the cold from outside to penetrate. However, the interior was just as frigid as the exterior. Figuring out how to increase the temperature was the challenge. But you can count on a "professional" for that. From my pockets I pulled out three or four newspapers. I burned these, one by one, on the floor of the car. The smoke drifted upward. Not a trace of the heat could get out, and, cozy and warm, I spent a wonderful night. I never woke up even once.

In the morning it was still snowing. While getting my feet ready for breakfast, I missed an eastbound freight train. Later that day I caught two other freight trains and was thrown off both of them. All afternoon no eastbound trains passed by. The snow was falling heavier than ever, but at dusk I climbed onto the first blind car of the cross-country train. As I jumped aboard the blind car from one side, someone else jumped on from the other side. It was the boy who had escaped from Oregon.

The front platform of a fast-moving train during a heavy snowstorm is far from pleasant. The wind cuts straight through you, hits the front of the car, and whips back around. When the train made its first stop and night had fallen, I walked up to the front and spoke with the fireman. I volunteered to shovel coal until the end of his shift, which would take us to Rawlins, and he agreed to let me help. My job was working out on the tender in the snow, breaking up chunks of coal with a heavy hammer and shoveling it forward to him in the locomotive cab. Since I didn't need to work continuously, I could step into the cab from time to time to warm myself up.

"Listen," I said to the fireman when I finally caught my breath, "there's a young boy back there on the first freight car platform. He's really cold."

The cabs on the Union Pacific engines are quite roomy, and we settled the kid into a cozy spot in front of the fireman's high seat, where the kid immediately fell asleep. We reached Rawlins at midnight. The snow was falling heavier than before. At this point, the engine was scheduled to enter the roundhouse and be replaced by a fresh locomotive. When the train came to a halt, I jumped down from the engine steps and landed right in the arms of a big man wearing a heavy overcoat. He started questioning me, and I immediately asked who he was. Without hesitation, he told me he was the sheriff. I backed down and listened carefully while answering his questions.

He started describing the boy who was still sleeping in the cab. I thought quickly. Clearly the family was tracking the boy, and the sheriff had received telegraphed orders from Oregon. Yes, I had seen the boy. I had first met him in Ogden. The date matched the sheriff's information. But the boy was still somewhere behind us, I explained, because he had been thrown off that same overland train that night when it left Rock Springs. And the whole time I was hoping that the boy wouldn't wake up, come down from the cab, and ruin everything for me.

The sheriff left me to go question the people in the shacks, but before he departed he said:—

"Bo, this town isn't the place for you. Do you understand? You need to get on this train and leave, and don't make any mistake about it. If I find you here after it's gone..."

I assured him that I wasn't in his town because I wanted to be there; the only reason I was there was because the train had made a stop; and that he wouldn't see me for dust with how quickly I'd leave his awful town.

While he went to question the homeless camps, I climbed back into the taxi. The young man was awake and wiping his eyes. I shared the news with him and suggested he ride the locomotive into the engine house. To make a long story short, the young man took the same cross-country route, riding on the front of the train, with directions to ask the fireman at the first station for permission to ride inside the engine. As for me, I got abandoned. The new fireman was young and hadn't become relaxed enough yet to break the company's rules against allowing homeless people in the engine; so he rejected my offer to shovel coal. I hope the young man had better luck with him, because spending all night on the front of the train in that blizzard would have meant certain death.

Oddly enough, even now I can't recall the specific details of how I ended up stranded in Rawlins. I remember watching the train disappear quickly into the blizzard, then making my way to a saloon to get warm. Inside, there was bright light and heat. The place was bustling with activity and completely open for business. Faro, roulette, craps, and poker games were all going strong, while some wild cowboys were having a rowdy good time. I had just managed to make friends with them and was drinking my first glass on their dime when a firm hand came down on my shoulder. I turned around and let out a sigh. It was the sheriff.

Without saying anything, he led me out into the snow.

"There's an orange special down there in the yards," he said.

"It's a damn cold night," I said.

"It leaves in ten minutes," he said.

That was it. There was no conversation. And when that orange freight train pulled away, I was hiding in the refrigerated cars. I was sure my feet would turn to ice before dawn, and during the final twenty miles approaching Laramie I stood straight up in the opening and jumped around to keep warm. The snowfall was too heavy for the railroad workers to spot me, and I wouldn't have cared if they had.

My twenty-five cents got me a hot breakfast in Laramie, and right after that I climbed aboard the blind baggage car of a cross-country train that was heading up toward the mountain pass through the spine of the Rocky Mountains. You don't usually ride the blind baggage during daylight hours, but in this fierce snowstorm at the peak of the Rockies, I figured the railroad workers wouldn't have the heart to throw me off. And I was right. They made it their routine to come check on me at every station stop to see if I had frozen to death yet.

At Ames' Monument, located at the peak of the Rocky Mountains—I can't recall the exact elevation—the shack appeared for the final time.

"Hey, Bo," he said, "do you see that freight train pulled off to the side over there to let us pass?"

I could see it. The object was on the adjacent track, just six feet from where I stood. In that fierce storm, if it had been even a few feet farther away, I would have missed it completely.

"Well, the stragglers from Kelly's Army are in one of those train cars. They have two feet of straw beneath them, and there are so many of them packed together that they keep the car warm."

His advice was solid, and I took it, though I was ready to jump off and catch the next train if the guy at the shack had been trying to trick me. But he'd been telling the truth. I found the car—a large refrigerator car with the sheltered door thrown wide open to let air flow through. I climbed up and went inside. My foot landed on someone's leg, then on another person's arm. The lighting was poor, and all I could see was a jumbled mass of arms, legs, and bodies tangled together. There had never been such a mess of people packed together. They were all lying in the straw, sprawled over, under, and around each other. Eighty-four tough drifters take up plenty of space when they're lying down. The men I stepped on weren't happy about it. Their bodies rolled beneath me like ocean swells, pushing me forward without my control. I couldn't find any straw to step on, so I ended up stepping on more people. They got angrier, and I kept moving forward. I lost my balance and dropped down suddenly. Unfortunately, I landed right on someone's head. The next instant he had pushed himself up on his hands and knees in fury, and I was sailing through the air. What goes up has to come down, and I crashed down on yet another man's head.

What happened after that remains quite hazy in my memory. It felt like being put through a threshing machine. I was tossed around from one end of the train car to the other. Those eighty-four hoboes worked me over until what little remained of me, through some miracle, managed to find a small bit of straw to rest on. I had been initiated, and into a lively group. For the rest of that day we traveled through the blizzard, and to pass the time it was decided that each man would tell a story. It was agreed that each story had to be a good one, and moreover, that it had to be a story no one had ever heard before. The punishment for failing was the threshing machine. Nobody failed. And I want to say right here that never in my life have I been part of such an amazing story-telling session. Here were eighty-four men from all over the world—I made eighty-five; and each man told a masterpiece. It had to be, because it was either masterpiece or threshing machine.

Late in the afternoon we reached Cheyenne. The blizzard was raging at its worst, and even though none of us had eaten anything since breakfast, no one wanted to venture out for dinner. We traveled through the storm all night, and the next day we found ourselves on the beautiful plains of Nebraska, still moving forward. We had left the storm and mountains behind us. The wonderful sun was shining over a cheerful landscape, and we hadn't eaten anything for twenty-four hours. We discovered that the freight train would arrive around noon at a town that, if I recall correctly, was called Grand Island.

We collected money and sent a telegram to the town officials. The message stated that eighty-five healthy, hungry hoboes would arrive around noon and that it would be wise to have dinner prepared for them. The authorities in Grand Island had two options available to them. They could feed us, or they could put us in jail. If they chose the latter, they would have to feed us regardless, and they wisely decided that providing one meal would be the less expensive option.

When the freight train pulled into Grand Island at noon, we were sitting on top of the train cars with our legs hanging down in the sunshine. Every police officer in town was there waiting for us. They organized us into groups and led us to different hotels and restaurants where meals had been prepared for us. We hadn't eaten anything for thirty-six hours, so we didn't need any instructions on what to do. Afterward, they marched us back to the railroad station. The police had wisely made the freight train wait for us. The train started moving slowly, and all eighty-five of us, spread out along the tracks, climbed up the side ladders. We "captured" the train.

We didn't have any dinner that night—at least the group didn't, but I did. Right around dinnertime, as the freight train was leaving a small town, a man climbed into the car where I was playing cards with three other hobos. The man's shirt was bulging in a suspicious way. In his hand he carried a beat-up quart container that had steam rising from it. I caught the smell of coffee. I handed my cards over to one of the hobos who was watching the game, and excused myself. Then, at the other end of the car, followed by jealous looks, I sat down with the man who had gotten on board and shared his coffee and the food handouts that had made his shirt bulge. It was the Swede.

At around ten o'clock in the evening, we reached Omaha.

"Let's get out of here," said the Swede to me.

"Sure," I said.

As the freight train approached Omaha, we prepared to jump off. However, the people of Omaha were prepared as well. The Swede and I clung to the side ladders, ready to leap down. But the freight train didn't come to a stop. Moreover, long lines of police officers, their brass buttons and badges gleaming under the electric lights, stood positioned along both sides of the railroad tracks. The Swede and I understood exactly what would happen to us if we dropped down into their waiting arms. We held tight to the side ladders, and the train continued rolling across the Missouri River toward Council Bluffs.

"General" Kelly, commanding an army of two thousand hoboes, had set up camp at Chautauqua Park, which was several miles distant. The group we had joined was General Kelly's rear guard, and after getting off the train at Council Bluffs, it began marching toward the camp. The night had grown cold, and strong wind gusts mixed with rain were both chilling and soaking us through. Numerous police officers were watching over us and directing us toward the camp. The Swede and I waited for the right moment and managed to escape successfully.

The rain started pouring down heavily, and in the complete darkness, unable to see our hands right in front of us, we groped around like two blind people searching for shelter. Our instincts guided us well, because we quickly discovered a saloon—not a saloon that was open and serving customers, not simply a saloon that had closed for the evening, and not even a saloon with a fixed location, but a saloon supported by large wooden beams, with rollers beneath it, that was being transported from one place to another. The doors were locked. A fierce gust of wind and rain swept down on us. We didn't hesitate. The door shattered, and we went inside.

I've experienced some brutal camping conditions in my day, "carried the banner" through hellish cities, slept in puddles of water, and rested in snow under just two blankets when the mercury dropped to seventy-four degrees below zero (which amounts to a modest one hundred and six degrees of frost); but I need to say right now that I never endured a harsher camp or spent a more wretched night than the one I experienced with the Swede in that traveling saloon at Council Bluffs. First off, the structure, elevated as it was above ground, had revealed countless gaps in the flooring through which the wind howled. Second, the bar stood empty; there wasn't any bottled liquor available to warm our bodies and help us forget our suffering. We lacked blankets, and wearing our soaked clothing, drenched to our skin, we attempted to rest. I curled up beneath the bar while the Swede positioned himself under the table. The gaps and cracks in the floor made sleep impossible, and after thirty minutes I climbed up onto the bar's surface. Shortly afterward, the Swede hauled himself up onto his table.

And there we trembled and begged for morning to come. I can say for myself that I shook until I couldn't shake anymore, until the trembling muscles wore themselves out and simply hurt terribly. The Swede whimpered and groaned, and every so often, through teeth that wouldn't stop chattering, he whispered, "Never again; never again." He whispered this phrase over and over, without stopping, a thousand times; and when he fell asleep, he continued whispering it in his dreams.

At the first light of dawn, we left our house of suffering and stepped outside into a thick, cold fog. We stumbled forward until we reached the railway tracks. I was heading back to Omaha to beg for breakfast; my friend was continuing on to Chicago. The time had come for us to part ways. Our trembling hands reached out to each other. Both of us were shaking from the cold. When we attempted to speak, our chattering teeth forced us back into silence. We stood there alone, cut off from the world; all we could make out was a short stretch of railroad track, with both ends disappearing into the swirling mist. We looked at each other without words, our joined hands trembling together. The Swede's face had turned blue from the cold, and I'm sure mine looked the same.

"Never again what?" I managed to say.

Speech struggled to emerge from the Swede's throat; then faint and distant, in a thin whisper from the very depths of his frozen soul, came the words:—

"Never again a hobo."

He stopped speaking, and when he continued, his voice became stronger and rougher as he declared his determination.

"I'm never going to be a homeless drifter again. I'm going to find work. You should do the same thing. Nights like this one cause rheumatism."

He squeezed my hand tightly.

"Goodbye, Bo," he said.

"Goodbye, Bo," I said.

The next moment, we were separated by the mist that swallowed us up. It was our final encounter. But here's to you, Mr. Swede, wherever you might be. I hope you landed that job.

Road-Kids and Gay-Cats

From time to time, I come across articles in newspapers, magazines, and biographical reference books that contain summaries of my life, where I discover, expressed in careful language, that I became a homeless wanderer in order to study sociology. This is quite considerate and well-meaning on the part of these biographers, but it isn't accurate. I became a tramp—well, because of the vitality that existed within me, because of the restless desire to roam that flowed through my veins and wouldn't allow me to stay still. Sociology was simply something that happened along the way; it came later, in the same way that getting soaked follows being dunked in water. I took to *"The Road"* because I couldn't stay away from it; because I didn't have enough money for train tickets in my pockets; because I was built in such a way that I couldn't spend my entire life working "one same shift"; because—well, simply because it was more natural for me to do so than not to.

This happened in my hometown of Oakland when I was sixteen years old. By that time, I had earned a remarkable reputation within my chosen group of adventurers, who knew me as the Prince of the Oyster Pirates. It's true that people just outside my circle—honest sailors from the bay, dock workers, yacht owners, and the legitimate oyster business owners—called me names like "tough," "hoodlum," "troublemaker," "thief," "robber," and various other unflattering terms. But all of this name-calling was actually flattering to me and only made me feel more important in the high position I held. At that time, I hadn't yet read "Paradise Lost," but later, when I came across Milton's line "Better to reign in hell than serve in heaven," I became completely convinced that great minds think alike.

It was during this period that a lucky series of circumstances led me on my first adventure along *The Road*. As it happened, there wasn't any work available in the oyster business at that moment; I had some blankets I needed to retrieve from Benicia, which was forty miles away; and at Port Costa, a few miles from Benicia, a stolen boat was anchored under the watch of the local constable. This boat belonged to a friend of mine named Dinny McCrea. Whiskey Bob, another friend of mine, had stolen it and abandoned it at Port Costa. (Poor Whiskey Bob! Just last winter his body washed up on the shore, riddled with bullet holes from an unknown shooter.) I had returned from "up river" some time earlier and told Dinny McCrea where his boat was located; Dinny McCrea immediately offered me ten dollars if I would bring it down to Oakland for him.

Time dragged by slowly, and I found myself with nothing to do. I sat on the dock and discussed the situation with Nickey the Greek, another unemployed oyster pirate. "Let's go," I said, and Nickey agreed. He was completely broke. I had fifty cents and a small boat. I spent the money and loaded the supplies into the boat: crackers, canned corned beef, and a ten-cent bottle of French mustard. (We really loved French mustard back then.) Then, late in the afternoon, we raised our small spritsail and set off. We sailed through the night, and the next morning, on the beginning of a magnificent flood tide with a favorable wind pushing us forward, we came racing up the Carquinez Straits toward Port Costa. There was the stolen boat, less than twenty-five feet from the wharf. We pulled up alongside and lowered our little spritsail. I told Nickey to go forward and pull up the anchor while I started untying the gaskets.

A man rushed onto the dock and called out to us. It was the constable. I suddenly realized I had forgotten to get written permission from Dinny McCrea to take his boat. I also knew the constable would want to charge at least twenty-five dollars in fees for seizing the boat from Whiskey Bob and looking after it since then. My last fifty cents had been spent on corned beef and French mustard, and the reward was only ten dollars anyway. I glanced quickly toward Nickey. He had the anchor positioned vertically and was pulling hard on it. "Pull it up," I whispered to him, then turned and yelled back to the constable. What happened next was that both of us started talking at once, our words crashing into each other in the air and creating complete nonsense.

The constable became more demanding, and I was forced to listen. Nickey was pulling on the anchor so hard I thought he might rupture a blood vessel. After the constable finished his threats and warnings, I asked him who he was. The time he spent explaining allowed Nickey to break the anchor free. I was making some rapid calculations. At the constable's feet, a ladder descended from the dock to the water, and tied to the ladder was a small boat. The oars were inside it. However, it was secured with a padlock. I staked everything on that padlock. I felt the wind against my face, noticed the movement of the tide, examined the remaining ties that held the sail, traced my gaze up the ropes to the pulleys and confirmed that everything was ready, then abandoned all pretense.

"Get her inside!" I yelled to Nickey, and jumped to the gaskets, loosening them and feeling grateful that Whiskey Bob had tied them with square knots instead of granny knots.

The police officer had climbed down the ladder and was struggling with a key at the padlock. The anchor was pulled aboard and the final rope was released at the exact moment the officer freed the small boat and grabbed the oars.

"Peak halyards!" I shouted to my crew, while simultaneously grabbing onto the throat halyards. The sail shot up quickly. I secured the line and rushed back to the tiller.

"Push her harder!" I yelled to Nickey when we reached the top.

The officer was just about to grab our back end. A gust of wind filled our sails, and we raced away. It was incredible. If I'd had a black flag with me, I definitely would have raised it in victory. The officer got to his feet in the small boat and ruined the beauty of the day with his colorful cursing. He also cried out for a weapon. You understand, that was another risk we had decided to take.

Anyway, we weren't stealing the boat. It didn't belong to the constable. We were simply taking his fees, which was how he made his corrupt money. And we weren't taking the fees for our own benefit, either; we were taking them for my friend, Dinny McCrea.

We reached Benicia within a few minutes, and shortly after that my blankets were loaded onto the boat. I moved the boat down to the far end of Steamboat Wharf, which gave us a good position to spot anyone who might be following us. There was no way to know for sure. Perhaps the Port Costa constable would call the Benicia constable. Nickey and I discussed our strategy. We stretched out on deck in the warm sunshine, feeling the fresh breeze against our faces while the incoming tide rippled and swirled around us. We couldn't possibly head back to Oakland until the afternoon, when the outgoing tide would start. However, we calculated that the constable would be watching the Carquinez Straits when the tide began to ebb, which meant our only option was to wait for the next outgoing tide at two o'clock the following morning, when we could sneak past our guardian in the cover of darkness.

So we stretched out on the deck, smoking cigarettes and feeling grateful to be alive. I spat over the side and measured the speed of the current.

"With this wind, we could ride this flood all the way to Rio Vista," I said.

"And it's fruit season on the river," said Nickey.

"And the water level on the river is low," I said. "It's the best time of the year to reach Sacramento."

We sat up and looked at each other. The magnificent west wind was flowing over us like wine. We both spat over the side and measured the current. Now I maintain that it was entirely the fault of that rising tide and favorable wind. They called to our sailor instincts. If it hadn't been for them, the entire sequence of events that would eventually put me on *The Road* would have fallen apart.

We didn't say a word, but untied our ropes and raised the sail. Our journey up the Sacramento River isn't part of this story. We eventually reached the city of Sacramento and docked at a pier. The water was excellent, and we spent most of our time swimming. On the sandbar above the railroad bridge, we encountered a group of boys who were also swimming. Between our swims, we lounged on the shore and talked. They spoke differently from the guys I was accustomed to hanging around with. It was a new way of speaking. They were road-kids, and with every word they spoke, the appeal of *The Road* gripped me more powerfully.

"When I was down in Alabama," one kid would begin; or, another, "Coming up on the C. & A. from K.C."; whereupon, a third kid, "On the C. & A. there aren't any steps to the 'blinds.'" And I would lie quietly in the sand and listen. "It was at a small town in Ohio on the Lake Shore and Michigan Southern," a kid would start; and another, "Ever ride the Cannonball on the Wabash?"; and yet another, "No, but I've been on the White Mail out of Chicago." "Talk about railroading—wait until you hit the Pennsylvania, four tracks, no water tanks, take water on the fly, that's really moving." "The Northern Pacific's a bad road now." "Salinas is on the 'hog,' the 'bulls' are 'hostile.'" "I got 'arrested' at El Paso, along with Moke Kid." "Speaking of 'handouts,' wait until you hit the French country out of Montreal—not a word of English—you say, 'Food, Madame, food, no speak the French,' and rub your stomach and look hungry, and she gives you a slice of salt pork and a chunk of dry 'bread.'"

I kept lying there in the sand, listening intently. These drifters made my small-time oyster stealing look completely insignificant. Every word they spoke revealed an entirely new world to me—a world of railroad tracks and freight car edges, hidden rides on trains and "side-door Pullmans," railroad police and brakemen, places to sleep and meals, arrests and escapes, robberies and migrant workers, newcomers and professionals. All of it promised Adventure. Fine then; I would take on this new world. I positioned myself among those wandering kids. I was every bit as strong as any of them, every bit as quick, every bit as bold, and my mind was every bit as sharp.

After the swim, as evening approached, they got dressed and headed into town. I went with them. The kids started "battering" the "main-stem" for "light pieces," or in simpler terms, begging for money on the main street. I had never begged before in my life, and this was the most difficult thing for me to accept when I first took to *The Road*. I held ridiculous ideas about begging. My belief system, up until that point, was that stealing was more honorable than begging; and that robbery was even more noble because the risk and punishment were correspondingly greater. As an oyster pirate I had already accumulated criminal convictions from the justice system, which, if I had attempted to serve them, would have demanded a thousand years in state prison. To steal was masculine; to beg was degrading and contemptible. But I evolved in the coming days just fine, just fine, until I eventually came to view begging as a delightful adventure, a battle of intelligence, an exercise for the nerves.

That first night, though, I couldn't manage it; and when the kids were ready to head to a restaurant for dinner, I wasn't able to join them. I had no money. I believe it was Meeny Kid who covered my meal, and we all dined together. But as I ate, I found myself thinking deeply about the situation. There's an old saying that the person who receives stolen goods is just as guilty as the thief; Meeny Kid had done the panhandling, and I was benefiting from it. I concluded that the receiver was actually much worse than the thief, and I resolved that this wouldn't happen again. And it never did. The following day I went out and begged for money just as skillfully as anyone else.

Nickey the Greek wasn't ambitious enough for life on *The Road*. He wasn't good at hopping trains, so one night he snuck aboard a barge and traveled downriver to San Francisco. I ran into him just a week ago at a boxing event. He's moved up in the world. He had a seat of honor right beside the ring. These days he manages boxers and takes pride in it. Actually, in his own small circle within the local sports scene, he's become quite a notable figure.

"No kid is a road-kid until he has traveled over 'the hill'"— that was the rule of *The Road* I heard explained in Sacramento. Fine, I'd cross over the hill and earn my place. "The hill," by the way, referred to the Sierra Nevada mountains. The entire group was heading over the hill on an adventure, and naturally I'd join them. This was French Kid's first experience on *The Road*. He had just run away from his family in San Francisco. It was up to him and me to prove ourselves. While I'm at it, I should mention that my old nickname "Prince" had disappeared. I had been given my "monica." I was now "Sailor Kid," and would later become known as "'Frisco Kid," once I had put the Rocky Mountains between myself and my home state.

At 10:20 PM, the Central Pacific overland train pulled out of the depot at Sacramento heading east—that specific time is permanently etched in my memory. There were about a dozen people in our group, and we spread out in the darkness ahead of the train, ready to hop aboard. All the local homeless kids we knew came down to see us off—and also to "ditch" us if they could manage it. That was their idea of a joke, and there were only about forty of them to pull it off. Their leader was an excellent homeless kid named Bob. Sacramento was his hometown, but he'd traveled the rails pretty much everywhere across the entire country. He pulled French Kid and me aside and gave us advice that went something like this: "We're going to try and ditch your group, understand? You two are weak. The rest of your crew can take care of themselves. So, as soon as you two catch a ride on a freight car, get on top of it. And stay on the roof until you pass Roseville Junction, where the police are hostile, arresting everyone they see."

The engine blew its whistle and the overland train pulled away from the station. There were three blind baggage cars on it— enough space for all of us. The dozen of us who were attempting to catch this train would have preferred to sneak aboard without being noticed; but our forty companions crowded on with the most incredible and brazen publicity and fanfare. Taking Bob's advice, I immediately "decked her," which means I climbed up onto the roof of one of the mail cars. There I lay flat, my heart pounding with extra beats, and listened to the commotion below. The entire train crew was at the front, and the process of throwing people off was happening quickly and aggressively. After the train had traveled about half a mile, it came to a stop, and the crew moved forward once more and threw off the remaining stowaways. I alone had successfully made it onto the train.

Back at the depot, surrounded by two or three members of the group who had seen the accident, lay French Kid with both legs severed. French Kid had slipped or lost his footing—that was all it took, and the train wheels had finished the job. This was my introduction to *The Road*. Two years passed before I encountered French Kid again and got a look at his "stumps." This examination was considered polite behavior. "Cripples" always appreciate having their stumps inspected. One of the fascinating spectacles on *The Road* is watching two cripples meet each other. Their shared disability provides plenty to talk about; they share the stories of how their injuries occurred, discuss what they understand about their amputations, offer critical opinions about their own surgeons and each other's, and conclude by stepping aside, removing their bandages and wrappings, and comparing their stumps.

But it wasn't until several days later, over in Nevada, when the crew caught up with me, that I found out about French Kid's accident. The crew itself showed up in terrible shape. They had been through a train wreck in the snow sheds; Happy Joe was walking on crutches with two crushed legs, and the others were tending to cuts and bruises.

In the meantime, I lay on the roof of the mail car, trying to remember whether Roseville Junction, the town Bob had warned me about, was the first stop or the second stop. To be certain, I waited to climb down to the platform of the blind baggage car until after the second stop. And then I didn't climb down at all. I was new to this way of life, and I felt safer where I was. But I never told the group that I stayed on the roof the entire night, all the way across the Sierra Nevada mountains, through snow sheds and tunnels, and down to Truckee on the other side, where I arrived at seven in the morning. Such behavior was shameful, and I would have become a laughingstock among everyone. This is the first time I have admitted the truth about that first journey over the mountains. As for the group, they decided that I was acceptable, and when I traveled back over the mountains to Sacramento, I was a fully accepted young hobo.

Yet I still had a lot to learn. Bob served as my mentor, and he was a decent guy. I recall one evening during the fair in Sacramento when we were hanging around and enjoying ourselves, and I ended up losing my hat in a brawl. There I stood in the street without a hat, and Bob came to my rescue. He pulled me aside from the group and explained what I needed to do. I felt somewhat hesitant about following his advice. I had just gotten out of jail after spending three days there, and I knew that if the police arrested me again, I would face serious consequences. However, I couldn't appear cowardly. I had crossed that line, I was running with the gang as a full member, and I needed to prove myself. Therefore, I took Bob's advice, and he accompanied me to make sure I carried it out properly.

We took our position on K Street, on the corner, I think, of Fifth. It was early in the evening and the street was crowded. Bob studied the hat of every Chinese man that passed by. I used to wonder how all the street kids managed to wear "five-dollar Stetson stiff-rims," and now I knew. They got them the same way I was going to get mine—from the Chinese. I was nervous because there were so many people around, but Bob was as cool as ice. Several times, when I stepped forward toward a Chinese man, all tense and ready to go, Bob pulled me back. He wanted me to get a good hat, and one that fit properly. Now a hat came by that was the right size but not new, and after a dozen unsuitable hats, along would come one that was new but not the right size. And when one did come by that was new and the right size, the brim was too wide or not wide enough. My goodness, Bob was picky. I was so worked up that I would have grabbed any kind of hat.

Finally, the hat appeared—the one hat in all of Sacramento that was meant for me. I could tell it was perfect the moment I saw it. I looked over at Bob. He quickly scanned the area for any police officers, then gave me a nod. I took the hat from the Chinese man's head and placed it on my own. It fit perfectly. Then I took off running. I could hear Bob shouting behind me, and I caught a quick glimpse of him getting in the way of the angry man and causing him to stumble. I kept running. I turned at the next corner, then around another. This street wasn't as busy as K Street, so I was able to walk calmly, catching my breath and feeling proud of both my new hat and my successful escape.

And then, suddenly, around the corner behind me, came the bare-headed Chinese man. With him were a couple more Chinese men, and following them were half a dozen men and boys. I sprinted to the next corner, crossed the street, and turned the following corner. I decided that I had surely outrun him, and I slowed down to a walk again. But around the corner behind me came that persistent man from Mongolia. It was the classic story of the hare and the tortoise. He couldn't run as fast as I could, but he kept at it, plodding along at a shuffling and deceptive trot, and wasting plenty of good breath on loud curses. He called all of Sacramento to witness the dishonor that had been done to him, and a good portion of Sacramento heard and followed at his heels. And I ran on like the hare, and always that persistent Mongolian, with the growing crowd, caught up to me. But finally, when a policeman had joined his followers, I gave it everything I had. I twisted and turned, and I swear I ran at least twenty blocks in a straight line. And I never saw that Chinese man again. The hat was excellent, a brand-new Stetson, fresh from the store, and it was the envy of the whole group. Furthermore, it was the symbol that I had accomplished what I set out to do. I wore it for over a year.

Street kids are decent little guys—when you catch them by themselves and they're explaining "how it all went down"; but trust me on this, be careful around them when they're running as a group. That's when they become wolves, and just like wolves, they can bring down even the toughest man. During those moments, they don't act like cowards. They'll throw themselves at a person and hang on with every bit of strength in their lean bodies until he's knocked down and defenseless. I've witnessed them do this more than once, and I'm speaking from experience. Their reason is typically theft. And be on guard for the "strong arm" technique. Every kid in the gang I traveled with had mastered it. Even French Kid had learned it before he lost his legs.

I have a vivid memory now of something I witnessed in "The Willows." The Willows was a cluster of trees on an empty lot near the train yard, just a five-minute walk from downtown Sacramento. It's nighttime, and the area is lit only by the faint glow of starlight.

I watch a muscular worker surrounded by a gang of homeless kids. He's furious and swearing at them, showing no fear, completely confident in his own power. He weighs around one hundred and eighty pounds with solid muscle, but he has no idea what he's facing. The kids are growling like animals. It's an ugly sight. They charge him from every direction, and he strikes out wildly, spinning around. Barber Kid stands next to me. As the man spins, Barber Kid jumps forward and executes the move. His knee drives into the man's back while his right arm wraps around the man's throat from behind, the bone of his wrist pressing hard against the jugular vein. Barber Kid throws all his weight backward. It's incredible leverage. On top of that, the man's breathing is cut off. This is the chokehold.

The man fights back, but he's already virtually powerless. The street kids swarm him from all directions, grabbing onto his arms, legs, and torso, and like a wolf at a moose's throat, Barber Kid clamps on and pulls him backward. The man topples over and disappears beneath the pile of bodies. Barber Kid shifts his position but never loosens his grip. While some of the kids are robbing the victim, others pin down his legs to prevent him from kicking and struggling. They seize this chance to pull off the man's shoes. As for the victim, he has surrendered. He is defeated. Moreover, with the powerful arm pressed against his throat, he can barely breathe. He makes terrible choking sounds, and the kids work quickly. They genuinely don't intend to kill him. Everything is finished. At a single command, all grips are released simultaneously, and the kids scatter in different directions, one of them carrying the shoes—he knows exactly where he can sell them for fifty cents. The man sits up and looks around, confused and helpless. Even if he wanted to give chase, running barefoot through the darkness would be futile. I stay for a moment and observe him. He touches his throat, making dry, rasping sounds, and jerks his head in an odd manner as if checking that his neck isn't broken. Then I slip away to rejoin the group, never seeing that man again—though I will always remember him, sitting there in the starlight, somewhat bewildered, a little scared, thoroughly disheveled, and making those strange jerking movements with his head and neck.

Drunk men are the primary targets of *The Road*-kids. They call robbing an intoxicated person "rolling a stiff," and wherever they find themselves, they constantly watch for drunk individuals. The drunk person serves as their preferred victim, much like a fly serves as the spider's chosen prey. Rolling a stiff often becomes an entertaining spectacle, particularly when the victim is completely helpless and intervention seems unlikely. During the initial attack, the victim's money and jewelry disappear immediately. Afterward, the kids gather around their target in a circle resembling a conference. One kid develops a desire for the victim's necktie and removes it. Another kid wants the undergarments, strips them off, and uses a knife to quickly cut through the sleeves and pant legs. Sympathetic hoboes might be invited to claim the coat and trousers, which prove too big for the kids to wear. Eventually they leave, abandoning their pile of worn-out clothing next to the unconscious victim.

Another vision comes to me. It is a dark night. My gang is walking along the sidewalk in the suburbs. Ahead of us, under a streetlight, a man crosses the street at an angle. There is something uncertain and aimless about the way he walks. The kids sense the opportunity immediately. The man is drunk. He stumbles across the sidewalk on the other side and disappears into the darkness as he takes a shortcut through an empty lot. No hunting cry goes up, but the pack throws itself forward in swift pursuit. In the middle of the empty lot it catches up with him. But what is this?— growling and strange shapes, small and shadowy and threatening, stand between the pack and its target. It is another pack of street kids, and in the tense standoff we discover that this is their prey, that they have been following him for a dozen blocks or more and that we are interfering. But this is the primitive world. These wolves are young wolves. (As a matter of fact, I don't think any of them was older than twelve or thirteen years. I met some of them later, and found out that they had just arrived that day from over the mountains, and that they came from Denver and Salt Lake City.) Our pack charges forward. The young wolves shriek and scream and fight like little devils. All around the drunk man rages the battle for control of him. Down he falls in the middle of it all, and the fight continues over his body in the same way the Greeks and Trojans fought over the body and armor of a fallen hero. With cries and tears and screams the young wolves are driven off, and my pack robs the victim. But I always remember the poor victim and his confused amazement at the sudden outbreak of fighting in the empty lot. I can see him now, barely visible in the darkness, swaying in bewildered wonder, good-naturedly trying to play the role of peacemaker in that chaotic brawl whose meaning he could not grasp, and the genuinely hurt look on his face when he, having done nothing wrong, was grabbed by many hands and pulled down into the thick of the crowd.

"Bindle-stiffs" are the preferred targets of road-kids. A bindle-stiff is a working vagrant who gets his name from the bundle of blankets he carries, called a "bindle." Since he works for a living, a bindle-stiff is typically expected to have some pocket money on him, and it's this small amount of cash that *The Road*-kids are after. The prime locations for finding bindle-stiffs are in sheds, barns, lumber yards, railroad yards, and similar places on the outskirts of a city, and the optimal time for hunting them is at night, when the bindle-stiff looks for these spots to unroll his blankets and get some sleep.

"Gay-cats" also fall victim to *The Road*-kid. In simpler terms, gay-cats are newcomers, greenhorns, fresh arrivals, or inexperienced travelers. A gay-cat is someone new to *The Road* who has reached manhood, or at least young adulthood. A boy on *The Road*, however, no matter how inexperienced he might be, is never called a gay-cat; he's a road-kid or a "punk," and if he travels with a "profesh," he's known as that person's "prushun." I was never a prushun because I didn't like being owned by anyone. I started as a road-kid and later became a profesh. Since I began so young, I essentially bypassed my gay-cat training period. For a brief time, while I was changing my nickname from 'Frisco Kid to Sailor Jack, some people suspected I might be a gay-cat. But once they got to know me better, those who had doubted me quickly changed their minds, and before long I had developed the unmistakable attitude and characteristics of a genuine profesh. And let it be understood, right here and now, that the profesh are the elite of *The Road*. They are the rulers and leaders, the dominant men, the natural aristocrats, the superior beings that Nietzsche admired so much.

When I returned over the hill from Nevada, I discovered that some river thief had taken Dinny McCrea's boat. (Something strange about this time is that I can't recall what happened to the small boat that Nickey the Greek and I used to sail from Oakland to Port Costa. I'm certain the police officer didn't confiscate it, and I'm sure it didn't come with us up the Sacramento River, and that's everything I remember.) With Dinny McCrea's boat gone, I was committed to *The Road*; and when I became weary of Sacramento, I said farewell to the group (which, in their characteristic manner, attempted to throw me off a freight train as I departed town) and began a journey down through the San Joaquin valley. *The Road* had taken hold of me and wouldn't release its grip; and later, after I had traveled to sea and pursued various other activities, I came back to *The Road* to take longer journeys, to become a "comet" and a professional, and to dive into the world of sociology that soaked me completely.

Two Thousand Corpses

A "stiff" is a tramp. I once had the chance to travel for a few weeks with a "push" that had two thousand members. This group was called "Kelly's Army." Throughout the rough and untamed West, all the way from California, General Kelly and his followers had seized trains; but they failed when they crossed the Missouri River and faced the refined East. The East had no intention whatsoever of providing free transportation to two thousand hoboes. Kelly's Army remained stranded helplessly for some time at Council Bluffs. The day I joined them, driven to desperation by the delays, they marched out to seize a train.

The scene was truly impressive. General Kelly sat atop a magnificent black horse, and with flags waving in the wind, accompanied by the martial music of fife and drum corps, his two thousand men marched company by company in two divisions, countermarching before him as they headed toward the wagon road leading to the small town of Weston, seven miles in the distance. Since I was the newest recruit, I found myself in the last company of the last regiment of the Second Division, and what's more, I was positioned in the very last rank of the rear guard. The army established camp at Weston next to the railroad tracks—actually beside multiple tracks, since two railway lines passed through the area: the Chicago, Milwaukee, and St. Paul Railroad, and the Rock Island Railroad.

Our plan was to catch the first train out, but the railroad officials blocked our move—and they won. There was no first train available. They shut down both railway lines and stopped all train service. Meanwhile, as we waited beside the inactive tracks, the good citizens of Omaha and Council Bluffs were taking action.

Plans were being made to organize a crowd, seize a train in Council Bluffs, bring it down to us, and give it to us as a gift. The railroad officials blocked that plan as well. They didn't wait for the crowd to act. Early on the morning of the second day, a locomotive with a single private car attached pulled into the station and moved onto a side track. At this sign that activity had returned to the dormant railways, the entire army formed a line alongside the track.

But life had never returned so dramatically to a dead railroad as it did on those two tracks. From the west came the sound of a locomotive whistle. It was heading in our direction, traveling east. We were also heading east. A wave of anticipation spread through our group. The whistle blew rapidly and intensely, and the train roared past at maximum speed. No hobo alive could have jumped aboard that train. Another locomotive whistled, and another train raced through at top speed, then another, and another, train after train, train after train, until finally the trains consisted of passenger cars, boxcars, flatcars, dead engines, cabooses, mail cars, wrecking equipment, and all the miscellaneous collection of worn-out and discarded railroad cars that accumulate in the yards of major railways. When the yards at Council Bluffs had been completely emptied, the private car and engine headed east, and the tracks fell silent forever.

That day passed, and the next one too, with nothing happening, while the two thousand hoboes remained lying beside the railroad tracks, getting pounded by sleet, rain, and hail. But that night, the good citizens of Council Bluffs outdid the railroad officials. A crowd gathered in Council Bluffs, crossed the river to Omaha, and joined forces with another crowd to raid the Union Pacific rail yards. First they seized a locomotive, then they put together a train, and finally the combined crowds climbed aboard, crossed the Missouri River, and traveled down the Rock Island railway to deliver the train to us. The railroad officials attempted to counter this move but failed, much to the deadly fear of the section boss and one section gang worker at Weston. Following secret telegraph instructions, this pair tried to derail our trainload of supporters by ripping up the railroad tracks. We happened to be suspicious and had posted guards. Caught in the act of sabotaging the train and surrounded by two thousand furious hoboes, the section gang boss and his helper expected to die. I can't recall what spared their lives, except perhaps it was when the train arrived.

It was our turn to collapse, and we did, severely. In their rush, the two groups had failed to secure a train that was long enough. There wasn't space for two thousand hoboes to travel. So the groups and the hoboes held discussions, bonded with each other, sang songs together, and separated, with the groups returning on their seized train to Omaha, while the hoboes set out the following morning on a one-hundred-and-forty-mile walk to Des Moines. Kelly's Army didn't start walking until it had crossed the Missouri, but after that point it never rode on trains again. This situation cost the railroads enormous amounts of money, but they were standing by their principles, and they emerged victorious.

Underwood, Leola, Menden, Avoca, Walnut, Marno, Atlantic, Wyoto, Anita, Adair, Adam, Casey, Stuart, Dexter, Carlham, De Soto, Van Meter, Booneville, Commerce, Valley Junction—the names of these towns flood back to me as I study the map and follow our path through the rich Iowa countryside! And what welcoming Iowa farming families we encountered! They came out with their wagons and transported our luggage; provided us with warm midday meals along *The Road*side; mayors from cozy small towns delivered welcoming speeches and sent us on our way; groups of young girls and women came out to greet us, and the good people turned out by the hundreds, linked arms, and walked with us down their main streets. It felt like carnival day whenever we arrived in town, and every day brought that same excitement, since there were so many towns to visit.

In the evenings, entire communities would flood into our camps. Each company gathered around its own campfire, and there was always something happening at every fire. The cooks from my company, Company L, were talented performers who provided most of our entertainment. In another section of the camp, the glee club would be singing—one of their standout voices was the "Dentist," who came from Company L, and we were extremely proud of him. He also extracted teeth for the entire army, and since these procedures usually took place during mealtime, our digestion was enhanced by the variety of excitement. The Dentist had no anesthetics, but two or three of us were always ready to volunteer to hold down the patient. Beyond the performances by the companies and the glee club, church services were typically conducted with local ministers leading them, and there was always plenty of political speechmaking. All these activities competed with each other; it was like a complete carnival midway. You can uncover a lot of talent among two thousand hoboes. I recall we had an excellent baseball team, and on Sundays we made it our routine to defeat the local teams. Sometimes we beat them twice on Sundays.

Last year, during a speaking tour, I traveled into Des Moines on a Pullman car—I'm talking about an actual Pullman, not a "side-door Pullman." As we approached the city's edge, I spotted the old stove factory, and my heart jumped. It was at that stove factory, twelve years earlier, that the Army collapsed and made a solemn vow that our feet were too painful and we wouldn't walk another step. We occupied the stove factory and informed Des Moines that we intended to remain permanently—we had walked into town, but we'd be damned if we were going to walk back out. Des Moines welcomed us, but this situation was pushing hospitality too far. Consider the numbers for a moment, dear reader. Two thousand drifters, consuming three full meals each day, creates six thousand meals daily, forty-two thousand meals weekly, or one hundred and sixty-eight thousand meals in the shortest month of the year. That's quite an undertaking. We had no funds. The burden fell on Des Moines.

Des Moines was in a desperate situation. We stayed in our camp, delivering political speeches, organizing religious concerts, extracting teeth, playing baseball and seven-up, and consuming our six thousand meals each day, with Des Moines footing the bill. Des Moines begged the railroad companies for help, but they remained stubborn; they had declared we wouldn't be allowed to travel by train, and that was final. Allowing us to ride would create a precedent, and they refused to set any precedents. Meanwhile, we continued eating. That was the frightening aspect of our circumstances. We were headed to Washington, and Des Moines would have needed to issue municipal bonds to cover all our train tickets, even at discounted rates, and if we stayed much longer, the city would have to issue bonds just to keep feeding us anyway.

Then a local genius came up with a solution to the problem. We wouldn't walk. That was fine. We would travel by water instead. The Des Moines River flowed from Des Moines to Keokuk on the Mississippi, covering a distance of three hundred miles. According to this local genius, we could travel along this river, and once we had boats, we could continue down the Mississippi to the Ohio River, then head up the Ohio, finishing with a brief overland journey across the mountains to Washington.

Des Moines organized a fundraising campaign. Community-minded residents donated several thousand dollars. They purchased lumber, rope, nails, and cotton for waterproofing in large amounts, and along the banks of the Des Moines River, an enormous shipbuilding period began. The Des Moines is actually a small waterway, given more importance than it deserves by being called a "river." In our vast western territory, it would be known as a "creek." The long-time residents doubted our success, insisting there wasn't sufficient water to keep us afloat. Des

Moines didn't mind, as long as they could get us to leave, and we were such confident optimists that we didn't worry about it either.

On Wednesday, May 9, 1894, we set off and began our enormous picnic adventure. Des Moines had escaped relatively unscathed, and the city certainly owes a bronze statue to the local mastermind who helped them out of their predicament. It's true that Des Moines had to cover the cost of our boats; we had consumed sixty-six thousand meals at the stove factory; and we packed twelve thousand extra meals in our food supplies as protection against starvation in the wilderness; but consider what it would have cost if we had stayed in Des Moines for eleven months rather than eleven days. Furthermore, when we left, we assured Des Moines that we would return if the river proved unable to carry us.

It was all well and good having twelve thousand meals in the commissary, and undoubtedly the commissary "ducks" enjoyed them; because the commissary quickly got lost, and my boat, for one, never saw it again. The company formation was completely broken apart during the river journey. In any camp of men there will always be a certain percentage of slackers, helpless individuals, ordinary folks, and go-getters. There were ten men in my boat, and they were the best of Company L. Every man was a go-getter. I was included in the ten for two reasons. First, I was as good a hustler as anyone who ever "hit *The Road*," and second, I was "Sailor Jack." I knew boats and boating. The ten of us forgot about the remaining forty men of Company L, and by the time we had missed one meal we quickly forgot about the commissary. We were self-sufficient. We went down the river "on our own," hustling our "grub," beating every boat in the fleet, and, sadly I must admit, sometimes taking possession of the supplies the farming folks had gathered for the Army.

For a good portion of the three hundred miles, we stayed anywhere from half a day to about a day ahead of the Army. We had succeeded in obtaining several American flags. Whenever we came near a small town, or whenever we spotted a group of farmers gathered along the riverbank, we hoisted our flags, identified ourselves as the "advance boat," and insisted on knowing what supplies had been gathered for the Army. We claimed to represent the Army, naturally, and the supplies were handed over to us. However, we weren't petty about it. We never took more than we could manage to carry off. But we did take the best of everything. For example, if some generous farmer had contributed several dollars' worth of tobacco, we took it. Similarly, we took butter and sugar, coffee and canned goods; but when the stores included sacks of beans and flour, or two or three butchered cattle, we firmly held back and continued on our way, leaving instructions to turn such supplies over to the commissary boats whose job was to follow behind us.

We certainly lived like kings, all ten of us! General Kelly spent a long time trying unsuccessfully to stop us. He dispatched two rowers in a lightweight, round-bottomed boat to catch up with us and end our pirate-like activities. They did catch up to us, but there were only two of them against our ten. General Kelly had given them authority to arrest us, and they informed us of this. When we showed that we had no intention of being taken prisoner, they rushed ahead to the next town to get help from the local authorities. We immediately went to shore and prepared an early dinner; then, under cover of darkness, we slipped past the town and its authorities.

I kept a diary during part of the journey, and as I look through it now, I notice one phrase that appears repeatedly: "Living fine." We truly did live well. We even refused to drink coffee made with water. Instead, we prepared our coffee using milk, and if I recall correctly, we called this delightful drink "pale Vienna."

While we were ahead, taking the best of everything, and while the supply officer was lost far behind, the main Army, traveling in the middle, went hungry. This was tough on the Army, I'll admit; but then, the ten of us were individualists. We had drive and ambition. We firmly believed that the food went to whoever got there first, the best pickings to the strongest. During one stretch the Army went forty-eight hours without food; and then it reached a small village of about three hundred people, whose name I don't recall, though I believe it was Red Rock. This town, following the custom of all towns the Army passed through, had formed a safety committee. Figuring five people per family, Red Rock had sixty households. Their safety committee was terrified by the sudden arrival of two thousand starving hoboes who lined their boats two and three deep along the riverbank. General Kelly was a reasonable man. He had no plans to burden the village. He didn't expect sixty households to provide two thousand meals. Besides, the Army had its treasury.

But the safety committee panicked. Their plan was to give "no encouragement to the invader," and when General Kelly tried to purchase food, the committee refused him. They claimed they had nothing to sell; General Kelly's money was worthless in their town. That's when General Kelly took action. The bugles sounded. The Army disembarked from the boats and assembled in battle formation on top of the riverbank. The committee was present to witness this. General Kelly's speech was short.

"Boys," he said, "when did you last eat?"

"Two days ago," they shouted.

"Are you hungry?"

A powerful roar of agreement from two thousand voices filled the air. Then General Kelly turned to the committee of safety:—

"You see, gentlemen, this is the situation we're facing. My men haven't eaten anything for forty-eight hours. If I let them loose on your town, I won't be held responsible for whatever happens. They're desperate. I offered to purchase food for them, but you refused to sell it to me. I'm now taking back my offer. Instead, I'm going to make demands. I'm giving you five minutes to make your decision. Either slaughter six steers for me and provide four thousand rations, or I'll turn my men loose. Five minutes, gentlemen."

The frightened safety committee took one look at the two thousand starving vagrants and gave up completely. They didn't even wait the full five minutes. They weren't willing to risk anything. The slaughter of the cattle and the gathering of the demanded supplies started immediately, and the Army had their meal.

And still the ten shameless individuals soared along ahead and collected everything they could see. But General Kelly put a stop to us. He sent riders down each riverbank, warning farmers and townspeople against us. They carried out their work thoroughly, that's for sure. The previously welcoming farmers greeted us with cold rejection. Additionally, they called the police when we tied up to the bank, and released the dogs. I know this firsthand. Two of those dogs caught me with a barbed-wire fence between me and the river. I was carrying two buckets of milk for the pale Vienna. I didn't damage the fence at all; but we drank common coffee boiled with ordinary water, and it was up to me to find myself another pair of pants. I wonder, gentle reader, if you have ever tried to quickly climb a barbed-wire fence with a bucket of milk in each hand. Ever since that day I have held a grudge against barbed wire, and I have collected information on the topic.

Unable to earn an honest living while General Kelly kept his two horsemen positioned ahead of us, we went back to the Army and started a revolution. It was a minor uprising, but it completely disrupted Company L of the Second Division. The captain of Company L refused to acknowledge us; he called us deserters, traitors, and scoundrels; and when he collected food supplies for Company L from the commissary, he wouldn't share any with us. That captain didn't value us, or he wouldn't have denied us food.

We immediately conspired with the first lieutenant. He joined our cause along with the ten men under his command, and in exchange we made him captain of Company M. The captain of Company L created an uproar. General Kelly, Colonel Speed, and Colonel Baker came down on us. The twenty of us held our ground, and our revolution was officially approved.

But we never used the commissary. Our resourceful crew members obtained better food supplies from the farmers. Our new captain, however, didn't trust us. He was never certain when he would see the ten of us again once we set off in the morning, so he brought in a blacksmith to secure his command. In the back of our boat, one on each side, two heavy iron eye-bolts were hammered in. Similarly, on the front of his boat, two massive iron hooks were attached. The boats were pulled together, end to end, the hooks were lowered into the eye-bolts, and there we were, locked together tight. We couldn't escape that captain. But we remained unstoppable. From our very chains we created an unbeatable system that allowed us to outperform every other boat in the fleet.

Like all great inventions, ours happened by accident. We discovered it the first time we got caught on a snag in some rapids. The front boat got stuck and held fast, while the back boat swung around in the current, using the front boat as a pivot point on the snag. I was at the back of the rear boat, doing the steering. We tried everything to push ourselves free, but nothing worked. Then I told the men from the front boat to jump into the back boat. Right away, the front boat broke free and floated clear, so its crew climbed back in. After that discovery, snags, reefs, shallow spots, and sandbars didn't scare us anymore. The moment the front boat hit something, its crew would leap into the back boat. Naturally, the front boat would then float over whatever was blocking it, and the back boat would hit the obstacle next. Like machines, the twenty men now crowded in the back boat would jump into the front boat, and the back boat would float past the obstruction.

The boats the Army used were all identical, mass-produced and cut to standard lengths. They were flat-bottomed vessels with rectangular designs. Each boat measured six feet in width, ten feet in length, and a foot and a half in depth. So when our two boats were connected together, I sat at the back steering a vessel twenty feet long, carrying twenty strong drifters who took turns at the oars and paddles, and packed with blankets, cooking equipment, and our own personal food supplies.

Still we gave General Kelly trouble. He had called in his horsemen, and replaced them with three police boats that traveled at the front and wouldn't let any boats pass them. The boat carrying Company M pressed close behind the police boats. We could have easily overtaken them, but it was against the rules. So we maintained a respectful distance behind and waited. We knew that ahead lay untouched farming country, unbegged and generous; but we waited. White water was all we needed, and when we came around a bend and saw rapids ahead, we knew what would happen. Crash! Police boat number one hits a boulder and gets stuck. Bang! Police boat number two does the same thing. Whop! Police boat number three meets the same fate as the others. Of course our boat does the same thing; but one, two, the men jump out of the front boat and into the rear boat; one, two, they leap out of the rear boat and into the front boat; and one, two, the men who belong in the rear boat are back in it and we're racing ahead. "Stop! you blankety-blank-blanks!" the police boats shout. "How can we?—blank the blankety-blank river, anyway!" we cry out pitifully as we rush past, caught in that relentless current that carries us on out of sight and into the welcoming farm country that restocks our private food supply with the best of its offerings. Once again we drink pale Vienna beer and understand that the food goes to the man who gets there first.

Poor General Kelly! He came up with another plan. The entire fleet set off ahead of us. Company M of the Second Division took its designated position in the line, which was at the very back. And it only took us a single day to completely ruin that specific plan. Twenty-five miles of treacherous water stretched out before us—nothing but rapids, shallow areas, sandbars, and rocks. It was this particular stretch of water that had made the longtime residents of Des Moines shake their heads in concern. Nearly two hundred boats entered the dangerous water ahead of us, and they crashed and got stuck in the most incredible way. We moved through that stranded fleet like wildfire through dry brush. There was no way to avoid the boulders, sandbars, and underwater obstacles except by getting out onto the shore. We didn't try to avoid them. We went straight over them, one after another, one, two, one, two, lead boat, rear boat, lead boat, rear boat, with everyone moving back and forth and back again. We made camp that night by ourselves, and relaxed in camp the entire next day while the Army fixed and repaired their damaged boats and slowly caught up to us.

There was no stopping our stubbornness. We set up a mast, loaded on the canvas (blankets), and traveled short hours while the Army worked overtime to keep us in sight. Then General Kelly turned to diplomacy. No boat could match us in the straightaway. Without question, we were the fastest group that ever came down the Des Moines. The ban on the police boats was lifted. Colonel Speed was placed aboard, and with this distinguished officer we had the honor of arriving first at Keokuk on the Mississippi. And right here I want to say to General Kelly and Colonel Speed that here's my hand. You were both heroes, and you were both men. And I'm sorry for at least ten percent of the trouble that was caused by the lead boat of Company M.

At Keokuk, the entire fleet was tied together to form one massive raft, and after being delayed by wind for a day, a steamboat pulled us down the Mississippi River to Quincy, Illinois, where we set up camp on the other side of the river at Goose Island. At this point, they gave up on the raft concept, instead connecting the boats in groups of four and adding decks on top. Someone mentioned to me that Quincy was the wealthiest town of its size in the entire United States. When I learned this, I was instantly seized by an overwhelming urge to try my luck begging. No genuine professional beggar could possibly ignore such a promising town. I made my way across the river to Quincy in a small dugout canoe, but I returned in a large riverboat, loaded down to the water line with everything I had gained from my begging efforts. Naturally, I kept all the money I had gathered, though I did pay for the boat rental; I also selected the best of the underwear, socks, discarded clothing, shirts, shoes, and hats; and after Company M had taken everything they wanted, there was still a substantial pile left over that went to Company L. Unfortunately, I was young and wasteful in those days! I told countless tales to the kind people of Quincy, and every story was effective; but since I began writing for magazines, I have often felt sorry about the abundance of stories, the wealth of fictional tales, that I squandered that day in Quincy, Illinois.

It was in Hannibal, Missouri, that our group of ten invincibles fell apart. This wasn't something we had planned. We simply scattered naturally. The Boiler-Maker and I slipped away in secret. That same day, Scotty and Davy made a quick escape to the Illinois shore, while McAvoy and Fish also managed their getaway. That accounts for six of the ten members; I have no idea what happened to the other four. To give you an idea of what life on *The Road* was like, I'm including the following excerpt from my diary covering the days after I left the group.

Friday, May 25th. Boiler-Maker and I departed from the camp on the island. We traveled to shore on the Illinois side using a small boat and walked six miles along the C.B. & Q. railroad to Fell Creek. We had traveled six miles out of our intended route, but we managed to board a hand-car and rode six miles to Hull's, located on the Wabash line. During our time there, we encountered McAvoy, Fish, Scotty, and Davy, who had likewise deserted from the Army.

"Saturday, May 26th. At 2:11 A.M. we jumped aboard the Cannonball as it slowed down at the crossing. Scotty and Davy were left behind. The four of us were abandoned at the Bluffs, forty miles down the line. In the afternoon Fish and McAvoy caught a freight train while Boiler-Maker and I were off getting something to eat."

"Sunday, May 27th. At 3:21 A.M. we caught the Cannonball and found Scotty and Davy riding the blind. We were all kicked off at daybreak in Jacksonville. The C. & A. railroad runs through here, and we're planning to take that one. Boiler-Maker left but didn't come back. I think he caught a freight train."

Monday, May 28th. The boiler-maker didn't show up. Scotty and Davy went off to sleep somewhere and didn't get back in time to catch the Kansas City passenger train at 3:30 A.M. I caught it and rode it until after sunrise to Masson City, which has 25,000 inhabitants. I caught a cattle train and rode it all night.

"Tuesday, May 29th. Arrived in Chicago at 7 A.M...."

And years later, in China, I was saddened to discover that the technique we used to navigate the rapids of the Des Moines—the one-two-one-two, head-boat-tail-boat method—wasn't something we had invented. I found out that Chinese river boatmen had been using a similar technique for thousands of years to handle dangerous waters. It's an effective method regardless, even though we can't claim credit for creating it. It passes Dr. Jordan's test of truth: "Does it work? Would you trust your life to it?"

Bulls

If the tramp were suddenly to disappear from the United States, widespread hardship for many families would result. The tramp allows thousands of men to make honest livings, educate their children, and raise them to be God-fearing and hardworking. I know this firsthand. At one time my father worked as a constable and hunted tramps to make a living. The community paid him a certain amount per person for all the tramps he could capture, and I believe he also received mileage fees. Money was always a pressing concern in our household, and the amount of meat on our table, a new pair of shoes, a day's excursion, or a textbook for school all depended upon my father's success in the hunt. I remember well the quiet anticipation and anxiety with which I waited each morning to discover what his previous night's work had accomplished—how many tramps he had brought in and what the likelihood was of securing convictions. And so it was that later, when I became a tramp myself and managed to escape some opportunistic constable, I couldn't help but feel sympathy for the little boys and girls back home in that constable's house; it struck me that in some way I was cheating those children out of some of life's good things.

But it's all part of the game. The hobo challenges society, and society's enforcers make their living off him. Some hoboes actually want to be caught by these enforcers—particularly during winter. Naturally, these hoboes choose communities where the jails are comfortable, where no labor is required and the meals are decent. Additionally, there have been, and most likely still are, police officers who share their arrest fees with the hoboes they bring in. This type of officer doesn't need to search for suspects. He simply whistles, and his targets walk straight into his hands. It's remarkable how much money gets made from penniless drifters. Throughout the South—at least during my time as a hobo—there are prison camps and plantations where farmers purchase the labor time of convicted hoboes, forcing these men to work. Then there are locations like the stone quarries in Rutland, Vermont, where the hobo faces exploitation, where the unused energy stored in his body, which he built up by begging from trains or going door-to-door for handouts, gets drained for that specific community's profit.

Now I don't know anything about the quarries at Rutland, Vermont. I'm really happy that I don't, when I think about how close I came to ending up there. Homeless people spread information to each other, and I first learned about those quarries when I was in Indiana. But when I reached New England, I kept hearing about them constantly, and always with warning signs attached. "They need workers in the quarries," the traveling vagrants would say, "and they never give a vagrant less than ninety days in jail." By the time I arrived in New Hampshire, I was pretty anxious about those quarries, and I avoided railroad police, security guards, and local officers like I never had before.

One evening I went down to the railroad yards at Concord and found a freight train assembled and ready to depart. I found an empty boxcar, slid open the side door, and climbed inside. I hoped to reach White River by morning; that would put me in Vermont and no more than a thousand miles from Rutland. But after that, as I traveled north, the distance between me and the point of danger would start to grow. In the car I discovered a "gay-cat," who showed remarkable nervousness when I entered. He mistook me for a "shack" (brakeman), and when he realized I was just a stiff, he started talking about the quarries at Rutland as the reason for the scare I had given him. He was a young country boy, and had only hopped trains over local sections of track.

The freight train started moving, and we settled down in one corner of the boxcar and fell asleep. A few hours later, when the train stopped, I woke up to the sound of the right-side door being quietly slid open. The inexperienced hobo kept sleeping. I didn't move, but I kept my eyes barely open, just enough to see through my eyelashes. A lantern appeared in the doorway, followed by a railroad worker's head. He spotted us and stared at us for a moment. I expected him to react angrily or shout the usual "Get out of here, you bum!" But instead, he carefully pulled back the lantern and very quietly slid the door shut. This seemed extremely strange and suspicious to me. I listened carefully and heard the latch quietly drop into place. The door was now locked from the outside. We couldn't open it from inside. One of our escape routes from the car was now blocked. This wouldn't work. I waited a few moments, then crawled over to the left-side door and tested it. It wasn't latched yet. I opened it, jumped down to the ground, and shut it behind me. Then I crossed over the couplers to the other side of the train. I opened the door that the railroad worker had latched, climbed back in, and closed it behind me. Both exits were accessible again. The inexperienced hobo was still sleeping.

The train began moving. It reached the next station. I could hear footsteps crunching on the gravel. Then the left door was flung open with a loud bang. The hobo woke up, and I pretended to wake up too; we both sat up and looked at the railroad worker and his lantern. He got straight to the point without wasting any time.

"I want three dollars," he said.

We stood up and moved closer to him to discuss the situation. We told him we were completely willing and eager to pay him three dollars, but we had to explain our terrible bad luck that prevented us from being able to do so. The conductor didn't believe us. He tried to negotiate with us. He said he would settle for two dollars. We apologized for being broke. He said insulting things, called us sons of toads, and cursed us thoroughly. Then he started making threats. He told us that if we didn't come up with the money, he'd lock us in and take us all the way to White River where he'd hand us over to the authorities. He also told us all about the stone quarries at Rutland.

The railroad worker thought he had caught us red-handed. Wasn't he watching the only door, and hadn't he just locked the door on the opposite side only minutes earlier? When he started talking about work gangs, the terrified inexperienced hobo began to slowly move toward the other door. The railroad worker laughed loudly and for a long time. "Don't rush," he said; "I locked that door from the outside at the last station." He was so certain the door was locked that his words sounded convincing. The inexperienced hobo believed him and felt hopeless.

The shack gave us his ultimatum. Either we had to come up with two dollars, or he would lock us up and hand us over to the constable at White River—which meant ninety days in the quarries. Now, dear reader, just imagine if that other door had been locked. Consider how fragile human life really is. For the lack of a single dollar, I would have ended up in the quarries and spent three months as a convict laborer. The same would have happened to the gay-cat. Don't worry about me, since I was a lost cause anyway; but think about the gay-cat. He might have emerged after those ninety days committed to a life of crime. And later he might have cracked your skull, yes your very skull, with a blackjack while trying to steal the money you were carrying—and if not your skull, then the skull of some other poor and innocent person.

But the door was unlocked, and only I knew it. The inexperienced hobo and I begged for mercy. I joined in the pleading and crying out of pure stubbornness, I suppose. But I did my best. I told a story that would have melted the heart of any fool; but it didn't melt the heart of that greedy money-grabbing railroad worker. When he became convinced that we didn't have any money, he slid the door shut and locked it, then waited a moment on the chance that we had tricked him and that we would now offer him the two dollars.

Then I really let loose. I called him a son of a toad. I called him all the other things he had called me. And then I called him a few additional things. I came from the West, where men knew how to curse, and I wasn't going to let any scruffy lowlife from some pathetic New England town outdo me in colorful and forceful language. At first the guy tried to laugh it off. Then he made the mistake of trying to respond. I unleashed even more, and I cut him down to nothing and rubbed salt in the wound with biting and fiery insults. My passionate outburst wasn't just for show or dramatic effect; I was genuinely angry at this despicable person who, for the lack of a dollar, would sentence me to three months of forced labor. On top of that, I had a strong suspicion that he was getting a kickback from the constable fees.

But I got him back. I hurt his feelings and wounded his pride to the tune of several dollars. He tried to intimidate me by threatening to come inside after me and beat me senseless. In response, I promised to kick him in the face while he was climbing in. I had the advantage of position, and he could see it. So he kept the door closed and called for help from the rest of the train crew. I could hear them responding and crunching through the gravel as they came to him. And the whole time the other door was unlocked, and they had no idea; and meanwhile the inexperienced hobo was nearly dying from fear.

Oh, I was quite the hero—with my escape route right behind me. I insulted the hobo and his companions until they threw the door open and I could see their furious faces in the glow of the lanterns. It was all very straightforward to them. They had us trapped in the train car, and they were going to come in and rough us up. They began their advance. I didn't kick anyone in the face. I yanked the opposite door open, and the inexperienced hobo and

I went out. The train crew chased after us.

We crossed over—if I recall correctly—a stone fence. But I'm certain about where we ended up. In the darkness I immediately tripped over a gravestone. The hobo tumbled over another one. Then we got the chase of our lives through that cemetery. The spirits must have thought we were really moving. The train crew thought so too, because when we came out of the cemetery and rushed across a road into a dark forest, the railroad workers gave up chasing us and returned to their train. A bit later that night the hobo and I found ourselves at a farmhouse well. We wanted a drink of water, but we spotted a small rope running down one side of the well. We pulled it up and discovered a gallon container of cream attached to the end. And that's as close as I got to the quarries of Rutland, Vermont.

When hoboes spread the word about a town, saying "the bulls are hostile," stay away from that place, or if you absolutely must go there, move through it quietly. There are certain towns where you always have to move through quietly. Cheyenne, on the Union Pacific railroad, was one such town. It had earned a nationwide reputation for being "hostile"—and this was entirely because of one man named Jeff Carr (if I'm remembering his name correctly). Jeff Carr could instantly assess what kind of "front" a hobo was putting on. He never bothered with conversation. In one moment he would size up the hobo, and in the next he would lash out with both fists, a club, or whatever else he could grab. After he had roughed up the hobo, he would run him out of town with a warning that things would be worse if he ever saw him again. Jeff Carr understood the system perfectly. North, south, east, and west to the farthest reaches of the United States (including Canada and Mexico), the beaten-up hoboes spread the message that Cheyenne was "hostile." Luckily, I never ran into Jeff Carr. I traveled through Cheyenne during a blizzard. There were eighty-four hoboes traveling with me at that time. Having so many people gave us confidence about most situations, but not when it came to Jeff Carr. The very mention of "Jeff Carr" overwhelmed our imagination, weakened our courage, and the entire group was terrified of encountering him.

It's rarely worth it to stop and try to explain things to police officers when they appear hostile. Making a quick escape is the best approach. It took me quite a while to figure this out, but the final lesson came from an encounter with a police officer in New York City. Ever since that experience, it has become second nature for me to run whenever I see an officer coming after me. This automatic response has become a fundamental part of my behavior, always ready to kick in at a moment's notice. I'll never be able to shake this habit. Even if I'm eighty years old, shuffling down the street with crutches, and a police officer suddenly reaches out toward me, I know I'd drop those crutches and sprint like a deer.

The final lesson in my education about bulls came on a sweltering summer afternoon in New York City. This happened during a week of blistering heat. I had developed the routine of lounging around in the morning, then spending my afternoons in the small park located near Newspaper Row and City Hall. It was in that area where I could purchase current books from street vendors—books that had been damaged during production or binding—for just a few cents each. Right there in the park were small stands selling wonderful, ice-cold, sterilized milk and buttermilk for a penny per glass. Every afternoon I would sit on a bench reading while indulging in a milk binge. I would consume anywhere from five to ten glasses each afternoon. The weather was unbearably hot.

So there I was, a quiet and bookish milk-drinking drifter, and look what I received in return. One afternoon I reached the park, carrying a newly purchased book under my arm and feeling an intense craving for buttermilk beneath my shirt. In the center of the street, directly in front of City Hall, I observed as I walked toward the buttermilk stand that a crowd had gathered. It was exactly where I needed to cross the street, so I stopped to discover what had drawn these curious onlookers together. Initially I couldn't see anything. Then, from the noises I heard and from a brief glimpse I managed to catch, I realized it was a group of street kids playing a marble game. Now this marble game isn't allowed on New York's streets. I was unaware of this fact, but I found out quite rapidly. I had stopped for perhaps thirty seconds, during which I had figured out what was attracting the crowd, when I heard one of the street kids shout "Cop!" The street kids understood the situation perfectly. They scattered. I remained standing there.

The crowd immediately dispersed and headed toward the sidewalks on both sides of the street. I made my way toward the sidewalk on the park side. There must have been fifty men from the original crowd who were going in the same direction. We were spread out loosely. I spotted the cop, a big policeman wearing a gray suit. He was walking down the middle of the street at a leisurely pace, just strolling along. I noticed casually that he changed direction and was heading at an angle toward the same sidewalk I was walking straight toward. He strolled along, weaving through the scattered crowd, and I realized that our paths would intersect. I was so unaware of any wrongdoing that, despite everything I'd learned about cops and how they operate, I suspected nothing. It never occurred to me that the cop was coming after me. Out of respect for the law, I was actually prepared to stop and let him pass in front of me. The stop did happen, but it wasn't my choice; it was also a backward stop. Without any warning, that cop had suddenly shoved me hard in the chest with both hands. At the same time, he verbally insulted my family lineage.

All my free American blood boiled. Every liberty-loving ancestor within me cried out in protest. "What do you mean?" I demanded. You see, I wanted an explanation. And I got one. Bang! His club crashed down on top of my head, and I was staggering backward like a drunk, the curious faces of the spectators swaying up and down like ocean waves, my precious book tumbling from under my arm into the dirt, the officer advancing with his club raised for another strike. And in that dizzying moment I had a vision. I saw that club falling many times upon my head; I saw myself, bloodied and beaten and hardened, standing in a police court; I heard charges of disorderly conduct, profane language, resisting an officer, and several other offenses, read aloud by a clerk; and I saw myself locked away on Blackwell's Island. Oh, I understood the game. I lost all interest in explanations. I didn't stop to retrieve my precious, unread book. I turned and ran. I was quite sick, but I ran. And run I will, until my dying day, whenever an officer begins to explain with a club.

Years after my wandering days had ended, while I was studying at the University of California, I went to the circus one evening. After the performance and concert concluded, I stayed behind to observe how the massive transportation machinery of a major circus operated. The circus was departing that same night. Near a bonfire, I discovered a group of young boys. There were approximately twenty of them, and as they spoke among themselves, I discovered they planned to run away with the circus. The circus workers, however, had no desire to deal with this collection of street children, so someone had called police headquarters to put a stop to their scheme. A team of ten officers had been sent to the location to arrest the boys for breaking the nine o'clock curfew law. The policemen encircled the bonfire and crept closer through the darkness. When given the signal, they charged forward, with each officer lunging at the children like someone reaching into a basket full of writhing eels.

Now I had no idea the police were coming; and when I witnessed the sudden appearance of brass-buttoned, helmeted officers, each one reaching out with both hands, all my inner strength and composure crumbled. Only the instinctive urge to flee remained. And I ran. I wasn't aware I was running. I wasn't aware of anything. It was, as I've mentioned, purely instinctive. There was no logical reason for me to run. I wasn't a vagrant. I was a citizen of that community. It was my hometown. I hadn't done anything wrong. I was a college graduate. I had even been mentioned in the newspapers, and I wore quality clothing that had never been slept in. Yet I ran—without thinking, frantically, like a frightened deer, for more than a block. And when I regained my senses, I realized I was still running. It took a deliberate act of willpower to stop my legs.

No, I'll never get over it. I can't help myself. When a police officer approaches, I run. Besides, I have an unfortunate tendency for ending up in jail. I've been arrested more times since I stopped being a hobo than when I actually was one. I set out on a Sunday morning with a young woman for a bicycle ride. Before we can even get outside the city limits, we're arrested for passing a pedestrian on the sidewalk. I decide to be more cautious. The next time I'm on a bicycle it's nighttime and my acetylene gas lamp is acting up. I tend to the weak flame carefully, because of the city ordinance. I'm in a hurry, but I ride at a crawling pace so I don't shake out the flickering flame. I reach the city limits; I'm beyond the reach of the ordinance; and I start speeding to make up for lost time. And half a mile down *The Road* I'm "nabbed" by a police officer, and the next morning I forfeit my bail in the police court. The city had sneakily extended its boundaries a mile into the countryside, and I had no idea, that was all. I remember my constitutional right of free speech and peaceful assembly, and I climb up on a soapbox to present the particular economic ideas that occupy my mind, and a police officer removes me from that box and escorts me to the city jail, and afterward I get out on bail. It's hopeless. In Korea I used to get arrested about every other day. It was the same situation in Manchuria. The last time I was in Japan I ended up in jail under the accusation of being a Russian spy. It wasn't my claim, but it landed me in jail all the same. There is no hope for me. I am destined to perform the Prisoner of Chillon routine eventually. This is prophecy.

I once hypnotized a police officer on Boston Common. It was past midnight and he had caught me red-handed; but before I finished with him he had handed over a silver quarter and given me the address of an all-night restaurant. Then there was a police officer in Bristol, New Jersey, who caught me and let me go, and heaven knows he had enough reason to put me in jail. I hit him harder than I'll bet he was ever hit in his life. It happened this way. Around midnight I jumped onto a freight train out of Philadelphia. The railroad workers threw me off. The train was pulling out slowly through the maze of tracks and switches of the freight yards. I jumped on her again, and again I was thrown off. You see, I had to jump on her from the outside, because she was a through freight with every door locked and sealed.

The second time I was kicked off, the brakeman gave me a stern talking-to. He told me I was putting my life in danger, explaining that this was a fast freight train that traveled at high speeds. I told him I was accustomed to traveling at high speeds myself, but he wouldn't budge. He said he wouldn't allow me to kill myself, so I had to get off the train. But I managed to catch her a third time, climbing on between the couplers. They were the smallest couplers I had ever seen——I'm not talking about the actual bumpers, the iron buffers that are connected by the coupling mechanism and that crash and scrape against each other; what I'm referring to are the crossbeams, like enormous brackets, that span across the ends of freight cars just above the couplers. When someone rides the couplers, they stand on these crossbeams, one foot on each side, with the couplers between their feet and just below.

But the beams or cleats I was standing on weren't the wide, sturdy ones that were typically found on boxcars during that era. Instead, they were extremely narrow—no more than an inch and a half wide. I couldn't even get half the width of my shoe sole onto them. Additionally, there was nothing for my hands to grip. While the ends of the two boxcars were there, those surfaces were completely flat and vertical. There were no handholds available. I could only press my palms flat against the car ends for stability. However, that would have been manageable if the cleats under my feet had been reasonably wide.

As the freight train pulled out of Philadelphia, it started picking up speed. That's when I realized what the railroad worker had meant by suicide. The freight train went faster and faster. It was a through freight, and nothing was going to stop it. On that stretch of the Pennsylvania Railroad, four tracks run side by side, and my eastbound freight didn't have to worry about passing westbound freights or being overtaken by eastbound express trains. It had the track all to itself, and it made full use of it. I found myself in an extremely dangerous position. I stood with just the edges of my feet on the narrow ledges, my palms pressed desperately against the flat, vertical ends of each car. And those cars moved constantly, each one moving independently, up and down and back and forth. Have you ever seen a circus performer standing on two galloping horses, with one foot on each horse's back? Well, that's exactly what I was doing, except with several crucial differences. The circus performer had reins to hold onto, while I had nothing at all; he stood on the full soles of his feet, while I balanced on just the edges of mine; he could bend his legs and body, drawing strength from the arch in his stance and achieving stability through a low center of gravity, while I was forced to stand completely upright and keep my legs straight; he rode facing forward, while I was riding sideways; and most importantly, if he fell off, he would only get a tumble in the sawdust, while I would have been crushed to pieces under the wheels.

And that freight train was definitely moving fast, roaring and shrieking as it swung wildly around curves, thundering over bridges, with one end of the car bouncing up while the other was jolting down, or jerking to the right at the same moment the other was lurching to the left, and with me praying and hoping the entire time for the train to stop. But it didn't stop. It didn't have to. For the first, last, and only time on *The Road*, I got everything I wanted. I left the bumpers behind and managed to climb out onto a side ladder; it was dangerous work, because I had never come across car ends that were so stingy with handholds and footholds as those car ends were.

I heard the engine's whistle blow, and I felt the train beginning to slow down. I knew the train wouldn't come to a complete stop, but I had decided to take my chances if it slowed down enough. The railroad tracks at this location curved around a bend, crossed over a bridge spanning a canal, and passed directly through the town of Bristol. This series of obstacles required the train to reduce its speed. I held tight to the side ladder and waited for my opportunity. I had no idea we were approaching the town of Bristol. I didn't understand what was causing the train to slow down. All I knew was that I desperately wanted to get off. I peered through the darkness, searching for a street crossing where I could safely jump. I was positioned quite far back on the train, and by the time my car reached the town, the engine had already passed the station and I could feel the train picking up speed once more.

Then came the street. It was too dark to see how wide it was or what lay on the other side. I knew I would need every inch of that street if I was going to stay upright after I jumped. I dropped off on the near side. It sounds simple. By "dropped off" I mean exactly this: First, while on the side-ladder, I pushed my body forward as far as possible in the direction the train was traveling—this was to create as much space as I could to build backward momentum when I swung off. Then I swung, swung out and backward, backward with every ounce of strength I had, and let go—while simultaneously throwing myself backward as though I planned to hit the ground with the back of my head. The entire effort was designed to counteract as much as possible the primary forward momentum the train had given to my body. When my feet hit the gravel, my body was leaning backward in the air at a forty-five-degree angle. I had managed to reduce some of the forward momentum, because when my feet made contact, I didn't immediately fall forward onto my face. Instead, my body straightened to vertical and started to lean forward. In reality, my body still carried significant momentum, while my feet, through contact with the ground, had lost all their momentum. This momentum that my feet had lost I now had to replace by lifting them as quickly as possible and running them forward to keep them beneath my forward-moving body. The result was that my feet pounded a rapid and explosive rhythm all the way across the street. I didn't dare stop them. If I had, I would have pitched forward. It was essential that I keep moving.

I was launched against my will, anxiously wondering what awaited me on the opposite side of *The Road* and praying it wouldn't be a brick wall or a telephone pole. At that very moment, I collided with something. What a nightmare! I glimpsed it just an instant before the crash—of all possible things, a bull, standing there in the shadows. We tumbled down together, rolling repeatedly; and the instinctive reaction was so strong in that wretched animal that at the moment of collision he stretched out and grabbed me and wouldn't release his grip. We were both stunned unconscious, and he clung to a very docile vagrant while he regained consciousness.

If that police officer had any imagination, he must have thought I was a traveler from other worlds, like someone from Mars who had just landed; because in the darkness he hadn't seen me jump from the train. In fact, his first words were: "Where did you come from?" His next words, before I had time to answer, were: "I've got half a mind to arrest you." This last comment, I'm convinced, was also automatic. He was really a good cop at heart, because after I had told him a "story" and helped brush off his clothes, he gave me until the next freight train to get out of town. I made two conditions: first, that the freight train be heading east, and second, that it shouldn't be a through freight with all doors sealed and locked. He agreed to this, and so, according to the terms of the Treaty of Bristol, I avoided getting arrested.

I recall another evening in that region when I narrowly avoided colliding with another bull. Had I struck him, I would have crushed him completely, since I was descending from overhead with nothing to slow me down, while several other bulls were just one leap behind me and trying to catch me. This is what occurred. I had been staying in a livery stable in Washington. I had a box stall and countless horse blankets entirely to myself. In exchange for such luxurious lodging, I cared for a group of horses every morning. I might still be there today if it weren't for the bulls.

One evening, around nine o'clock, I returned to the stable to go to bed and discovered a dice game in full swing. It had been a market day, and all the Black men had money. It would be helpful to explain the layout of the place. The livery stable faced two streets. I entered through the front, walked through the office, and came to the alley between two rows of stalls that ran the length of the building and opened onto the other street. Halfway down this alley, beneath a gas lamp and between the rows of horses, were about forty Black men. I joined them as a spectator. I was broke and couldn't play. A man was rolling the dice and winning. He was riding his luck, and with each roll the total stake doubled. All kinds of money lay on the floor. It was captivating. With each roll, the odds increased tremendously against the man making another successful pass. The excitement was intense. And just then there came a thundering crash on the big doors that opened onto the back street.

A few of the Black men ran in the opposite direction. I stopped running for a moment to grab some of the money scattered on the floor. This wasn't stealing—it was simply what everyone did. Every person who hadn't fled was grabbing what they could. The doors burst open and swung inward, and through them rushed a squad of police officers. We surged the other way. The office was dark, and the narrow doorway wouldn't allow all of us to escape to the street at once. Everything became jammed up. One Black man dove through the window, taking the window frame with him, followed by others. Behind us, the officers were arresting people. A large Black man and I both rushed toward the door at the same time. He was bigger than me, so he pushed me aside and got through first. The next moment a club struck him on the head and he dropped like a fallen animal. Another squad of officers was waiting outside for us. They knew they couldn't stop the stampede with their hands alone, so they were swinging their clubs. I stumbled over the fallen man who had pushed past me, dodged a swing from a club, dove between an officer's legs, and broke free. And then how I ran! There was a thin mixed-race man just ahead of me, and I matched his pace. He knew the town better than I did, and I realized that following his route meant safety. But he, on the other hand, thought I was a pursuing officer. He never looked back. He just kept running. My stamina was good, and I stayed with his pace and nearly exhausted him. Eventually he stumbled weakly, fell to his knees, and gave up, thinking I had caught him. And when he realized I wasn't an officer, the only thing that saved me was that he had no energy left to fight.

That's why I left Washington—not because of the mulatto, but because of the police officers. I went down to the train station and jumped onto the first blind car of a Pennsylvania Railroad express. Once the train picked up speed and I saw how fast we were going, doubt hit me. This was a four-track railway, and the locomotives refilled their water tanks while moving. Fellow hoboes had warned me long ago never to ride the first blind car on trains where the engines took on water while in motion. Now let me break this down. Between the railroad tracks are shallow metal channels filled with water. When the locomotive passes over them at full speed, a kind of scoop drops down into the channel. What happens is that all the water in the channel shoots up through the scoop and fills the locomotive's water tank.

Somewhere between Washington and Baltimore, as I sat on the platform of the blind baggage car, a light mist started to fill the air. It caused no trouble. Ah, I thought to myself; this whole idea about taking on water while moving being dangerous for hobos on the first blind car is just nonsense. What harm could this little spray possibly do? Then I started to admire the engineering. This was real railroading! Talk about your basic Western railroad operations—and just then the water tender overflowed, even though the train hadn't reached the end of the water trough yet. A massive wave of water cascaded over the back of the tender and crashed down on me. I was drenched completely, as soaked as if I had been thrown into the ocean.

The train arrived in Baltimore. Following the typical pattern in major Eastern cities, the railroad tracks ran below street level at the bottom of a large excavated channel. When the train entered the illuminated station, I made myself as inconspicuous as possible on the blind car. However, a railroad detective spotted me and began pursuing me. Two additional officers joined the chase. I had moved beyond the station and continued running straight down the tracks. I found myself caught in a kind of trap. The steep walls of the excavated channel rose on both sides of me, and I understood that if I attempted to scale them and failed, I would tumble back down into the hands of the railroad police. I kept running, examining the channel walls for a suitable spot to climb out. Finally, I discovered such a location. It appeared just after I had passed beneath a bridge that carried a street across the channel at ground level. I scrambled up the steep incline, grasping with both hands and feet. The three railroad detectives were climbing up directly behind me.

At the top, I discovered myself in an empty lot. On one side stood a low wall that divided it from the street. There wasn't time for a detailed examination. They were right behind me. I made my way to the wall and jumped over it. And that's exactly where I received the shock of my life. People usually assume that one side of a wall is the same height as the other side. But this wall was different. You see, the empty lot sat much higher than the street level. On my side the wall was low, but on the other side—well, as I came flying over the top, completely airborne, it felt like I was dropping feet-first, straight into a chasm. There below me, on the sidewalk, beneath the glow of a street lamp was a bull. I think it was nine or ten feet down to the sidewalk; but in the moment of surprise while suspended in mid-air it felt like twice that distance.

I straightened myself in the air and came down. At first I thought I was going to land right on top of the bull. My clothing brushed against him as my feet hit the sidewalk with tremendous force. It was amazing he didn't collapse from shock, since he hadn't heard me approaching. It was like that man-from-Mars trick all over again. The bull definitely jumped. He pulled back from me the way a horse reacts to a car, and then he lunged toward me. I didn't pause to offer any explanations. I left that job to the people chasing me, who were climbing over the wall quite cautiously. But I certainly got myself a chase. I ran up one street and down another, weaved around corners, and finally managed to escape.

After spending some of the money I'd won from the dice game and killing an hour of time, I returned to the railroad cut, just beyond the lights of the train station, and waited for a train. My blood had cooled down, and I shivered miserably in my wet clothes. Finally a train pulled into the station. I stayed hidden in the darkness, and successfully climbed aboard when it departed, making sure this time to reach the second car behind the engine. No more getting soaked while jumping onto moving trains for me. The train traveled forty miles to its first stop. I got off at a well-lit station that looked strangely familiar. I was back in Washington. Somehow, during the excitement of escaping Baltimore, running through unfamiliar streets, dodging and turning and backtracking, I had gotten completely turned around. I had caught the train going in the wrong direction. I had lost a night's sleep, I had been drenched to the skin, I had been chased for my life; and for all my troubles I was back where I had started. Oh, no, life on *The Road* is not all fun and games. But I didn't return to the stable. I had done some pretty successful stealing, and I didn't want to settle accounts with those men. So I caught the next train out, and ate my breakfast in Baltimore.

THE END

Thank You For Reading

You've Just Read a Piece of the Greatest Library Ever Rebuilt

Thank you for reading.

This book is one of thousands we're restoring, reimagining, and translating as part of the **Modern Library of Alexandria** — a global movement to preserve and share humanity's most important ideas.

What was once lost to fire and time is now rising again — not just as memory, but as living, breathing knowledge, freely accessible to all.

What You Can Do Next:

- **Keep Reading.**

  Discover more legendary works — in beautiful print, audiobook, or digital form — at LibraryofAlexandria.com.

- **Build Your Own Library.**

  Every title is available as a paperback, hardcover, or collectible boxset — at true printing cost. Craft a personal library worthy of display.

- **Spread the Light.**

  Share this book. Tell others about the movement. Help us translate every timeless work into every language, so no reader is ever left behind.

By finishing this book, you've already taken part in something extraordinary.

Join us at LibraryofAlexandria.com

Together, we're rebuilding the greatest library the world has ever known.

With appreciation,

The Modern Library of Alexandria Team

Visit:
www.libraryofalexandria.com
Or scan the code below:

www.ingramcontent.com/pod-product-compliance
Lightning Source LLC
Chambersburg PA
CBHW011356010726
47494CB00008B/2343